Praise for *Loving and Living Your Way Through Grief*

"When you're hurting, *Loving and Living Your Way Through Grief* serves as a steadfast guide to ease your deep sorrow, open your heart to joy, and restore your life after loss. Emily Thiroux Threatt not only teaches you how to use love and joy to cope with loss, but also offers many practical tools and useful suggestions to rebuild your shattered world. From journaling to practicing gratitude to setting intentions, you'll find support, understanding, and comfort whether you're new to grief or have been living with loss for years. Filled with insight, wisdom, and relatable stories, this resource shares everything you need to know to start living again with joy, meaning, and love after loss."

> —**Chelsea Hanson**, author of *The Sudden Loss Survival Guide:
> 7 Essential Practices for Healing Grief*

"*Loving and Living Your Way Through Grief* is a deeply transformative book. Emily's poignant experiences of loss captivate the reader and takes them on a journey of inner strength and hope. She has distilled her lifetime of experiences into timeless wisdom and strategies to help others work through their own losses and to know they are not alone. As a clinical psychologist and psychoanalyst with over thirty-five years of experience, I can highly recommend this book to anyone who has or is facing challenging life circumstances."

> —**Tony Toneatto, PhD**, professor at the University of
> Toronto, Canada

T0161735

"An insightful, riveting, thoughtful, and thoroughly engaging work on finding joy while experiencing grief. Inspired by her personal experience, Emily Thiroux Threatt generously and lovingly offers a practical yet spiritual guide for loving and living your way through a process no one welcomes but all must at some time traverse. *Loving and Living Your Way Through Grief* provides a wealth of reader-friendly support, guidance, encouragement and acknowledgement for implementation of its wise, workable recommendations for navigating through the loss of a loved one. Spiritual practice, common sense, and uncommon wisdom fill these pages. Letters and lists, stages and steps, principles and processes address, inspire, and motivate feeling how you feel, living in the moment, surviving and thriving—all in the midst of your grief. A wondrous and welcome addition to your library of living and loving through loss, this book is to be savored, treasured and kept close at hand and heart as needed, desired and required. A true gift to a grieving heart."

    —Rev. Greta Sesheta, 7-Pointer Star Ministries

"We all know that grief is a long process, but I find few resources that are structured to walk us through that first year of loss in both an empathetic and a constructive way. Reading this book is like sitting down with Emily on her back porch in Maui, sipping tea and talking about life. While it's so easy to self-isolate when grieving, this book might be the first 'friend' you invite back in. You'll find kind, gentle words, as well as practical resources to help you on your journey."

    —Danica Thurber, certified therapeutic art life coach,
    Project Grief

"There are many reasons I love this book. Two of them are that it is easy to read and it contains many easy-to-do ideas to ease your loss. I wish it was available when my wife died. It wasn't then, but it is now. Don't miss a chance to get this heartfelt handbook of healing. It is a godsend."

—**Allen Klein**, author of *Embracing Life After Loss*

"Threatt's personal experience with the deaths of husbands, parents, and other loved ones equipped her well to author this primer in navigating the territory of grief. She recognizes the uniqueness of each person's grief and offers a smorgasbord of practical suggestions to help people along their individual paths. This book is quite timely, given the current pandemic which has left immeasurable grief in its wake."

—**Brooke A. Brown, PhD**, founder of Nā Keiki O Emalia, a nonprofit foundation which provides support to grieving children, teens, and their families to help them heal after the death of a loved one

"Study this book and utilize its practices. It will support you in taking back your mind, heart, and life from merely coping and getting by after loss, to living and loving—freely and unconditionally—as you're meant to."

—**Michael Bernard Beckwith**, author of *Life Visioning, The Answer Is You*, and others

"Emily Thiroux Threatt's *Loving and Living Your Way Through Grief* vibrates with a gentleness and compassion that I didn't realize I needed until I read it. Thank you, Emily."

—**Laurie Kilmartin**, comedian, author of *Dead People Suck* and writer for television's *Conan*

LOVING
and
LIVING
your way
THROUGH
GRIEF

LOVING
and
LIVING
your way
THROUGH
GRIEF

A Comprehensive Guide to
Reclaiming and Cultivating Joy and
Carrying on in the Face of Loss

By **Emily Thiroux Threatt**

Mango Publishing

CORAL GABLES

For permission requests, please contact the publisher at:
Mango Publishing Group
2850 S Douglas Road, 2nd Floor
Coral Gables, FL 33134 USA
info@mango.bz

For special orders, quantity sales, course adoptions and corporate sales, please email the publisher at sales@mango.bz. For trade and wholesale sales, please contact Ingram Publisher Services at customer.service@ingramcontent.com or +1.800.509.4887.

Loving and Living Your Way Through Grief: A Comprehensive Guide to Reclaiming and Cultivating Joy and Carrying on in the Face of Loss

Library of Congress Cataloging-in-Publication number: 2020949682
ISBN: (print) 978-1-64250-482-8, (ebook) 978-1-64250-483-5
BISAC category code SEL010000, SELF-HELP / Death, Grief, Bereavement

Printed in the United States of America

To the memory of my husbands, the loves of my life,
Jacques Thiroux
Rev. Ron Threatt

and the memory of my parents,
Orville and Hazel Lofton

Table of Contents

Foreword 11

Preface 14

Introduction 15

Chapter 1: **Lori's Letter** 25

Chapter 2: **Wrap Yourself in Love** 31

Chapter 3: **Feeling How You Feel** 37

Chapter 4: **Meditation** 43

Chapter 5: **Cocooning** 51

Chapter 6: **Loss** 57

Chapter 7: **Gratitude** 67

Chapter 8: **Self-Love** 73

Chapter 9: **Judgment** 81

Chapter 10: **Being Social** 89

Chapter 11: **Loneliness** 97

Chapter 12: **Joy** 103

Chapter 13: **The Stages of Grief** 111

Chapter 14: **Your Memories** 121

Chapter 15: **What Others Say** 133

Chapter 16: **Grief Is Healthy** 141

Chapter 17: **Tell Your Story** 153

Chapter 18: **Feeling Guilty** 163

Chapter 19: **Living in the Moment** 171

Chapter 20: **Following Your Bliss** 183

Chapter 21: **Accepting Invitations** 191

Chapter 22: **Transformation and Preparation** 199

Chapter 23: **Regret** 207

Chapter 24: **Becoming Aware** 215

Chapter 25: **Forgiveness** 225

Chapter 26: **Surviving and Thriving** 233

Afterword 237

Gratitude 239

About the Author 241

Foreword

Oftentimes, when a loved one dies, its sting can catch and hold us in a web of grief, loss, and even despair. As we tend to feel emotionally, soulfully, and even physically connected to our loved ones, these relationships often provide us with a profound sense of intimacy, comfort, and stasis, and can become the very foundation of who we believe we are. So, when they die, it can feel like pieces of our very identity have been snatched away, and the sense of loss is felt at the core of our being. Such feelings of loss often engender variations of the questions: *Why did this have to happen? Why did they have to leave? Who am I without them in my life? How am I supposed to live without them? What will I do?* Although such inquiries are typically borne of grief, when understood within a spiritual context, they can provide the opportunity for intense inner reflection and contemplation, and ultimately, transformation.

You see, not only is it possible to live happily and thrive after a loved one transitions, it is *required* of us as the eternal and expansive beings we actually are. Many of us have been conditioned to experience our earthly lives and relationships through our physical senses, to what and whom we can see, hear, and touch, so we are attached to this as the ideal experience. However, limiting our ability to feel and share love, intimacy, beauty, and bliss to only that which we can see, hear, and touch, literally blunts our awareness of our innate cosmic connection to our supernal reality in which these conditions actually exist.

It would support us immensely to remember that, while the terms of our relationship with our loved ones may change, the nature and reality of it doesn't, as Real Love, in its eternality, can never "die." To grasp this, we must rethink and process *how* we relate, *how* we love, and what actually constitutes an unconditionally loving relationship from within. *Loving and Living Your Way Through Grief* can be your trusted resource and guide through that process back to recognizing Real Love. Emily is a living example of someone who, instead of merely coping with her grief and sorrow, transcended those experiences to live an authentically peaceful and joyful life through spiritual self-discovery.

I met Emily through her husband and my good friend, Rev. Ron Threatt, when they attended Agape International Spiritual Center while living in Los Angeles. I saw Emily's spiritual growth through her right use of spiritual principles in a very powerful way. When Ron passed, you could see her simultaneously experiencing sadness and loss and embracing the spiritual principles that ultimately pulled her through. Through her spiritual practice and self-realization, Emily was able to ultimately alchemize her sadness into a deeper awareness of love, earning her invaluable revelations, insights, and the wisdom that comes with spiritual transformation that both allows *and* calls her to minister to and support others who are grieving from loss—not only loss of a loved one, but loss of any kind.

Study this book and utilize its practices. It will support you in taking back your mind, heart, and life from merely coping and getting by after loss, to living and loving—freely and unconditionally—as you're meant to. As Emily says, "By approaching this process with an open heart and open arms, we can all learn, love, share and be the best that we can be."

Peace & Richest Blessings,

Michael Bernard Beckwith

Founder & Spiritual Director, Agape International Spiritual Center

Author, *Life Visioning* and *Spiritual Liberation*

Preface

At the end of each chapter in *Loving and Living Your Way Through Grief*, you will find suggested practices. When you do these practices, keep in mind that our world is dealing with a pandemic and its aftereffects. Because of this, use whatever methods are necessary to stay safe, such as social distancing and wearing a mask. Take good care of yourself. I care about you.

Introduction

In life, we all experience loss, whether it is when a loved one dies, a job is lost, a marriage ends, a house burns down, a loss of a pregnancy, a nest egg is lost, our beloved pet dies, or when anyone or anything that we loved is no longer in our lives. We joyfully anticipate the birth of a baby and spending time reading books, taking classes, preparing a nursery, and attending baby showers. But when loss occurs, we are generally unprepared. But just like birth, the more we prepare for loss, the easier it will be to go through the process and everything that surrounds it. Unfortunately, we don't usually make any preparations for the reality of loss. Many of us ignore it, or we just assume loss won't happen to us, so when loss occurs, we tend to be totally unprepared. Most of us live in some state of denial until loss actually occurs, and then we are lost. Immediately, our whole world stands still as we try to absorb what has happened, and at the same time not being entirely sure of how we can begin to live again.

I know what this poignant moment of loss feels like from my own personal experiences of losing many loved ones and dealing with other kinds of losses over the years. These experiences have led me to becoming a guide for others who need support on their journey as they start to live again and become open to loving and living again.

The Unfolding of My Personal Journey

In reflecting on my life, my calling and purpose seemed to appear early in my youth. When I was fourteen years old, I started going on ambulance calls because my family acquired an ambulance company. Back in the day, it was permissible for a fourteen-year-old to go on ambulance calls, so I went on those calls, where crisis and death was a frequent experience. Later, I became a licensed vocational nurse, where I also dealt often with crisis and with dying patients and their families. My parents, all of my aunts and uncles, my brother-in-law, and many friends have all transitioned. These experiences taught me of the inevitability of crisis and death, including my own.

Perhaps the most difficult losses that I have experienced are the deaths of two wonderful husbands. I had two very different experiences with grieving them. When I married Jacques, a man twenty-one years older than me, my friends questioned my decision, pointing out what I was in for. Of course, I ignored their advice because we were so happy and in love. We had a marvelous five years before his health started to fall apart. First, he was diagnosed with diabetes, then he had coronary artery bypass graft surgery where they did seven bypass grafts. I didn't even know there were that many places to bypass. The surgery truly gave him a fresh start. He lost weight, stopped having to take insulin injections, went to cardiac rehabilitation, and went for regular walks, on which he stopped to smell the roses. Joy came back into our lives. He was a college professor, a bioethicist whose specialty was the art of living and dying. His most popular class was required for all nursing students and was about dealing with death.

A few years passed and he gained weight, stopped exercising, and went back on insulin. I encouraged him to take care of himself, but he was busy enjoying life and spending time acting and singing in local theater productions. Then, he told me that he felt like he had before his heart surgery, so we went to the doctor right away. His new cardiologist insisted that he had a dangerously blocked artery and had to have another surgery immediately. When he had his last surgery, I had the chance to actually view the film of his angiogram where the doctor pointed out to me his main problem, which was a blockage called "the widow maker," a term I'll never forget. My husband asked his new doctor if he could see the angiogram, since he hadn't gotten to see it last time. We went into a small, dark room with his doctor and another cardiac research physician, who was a friend of ours. The new doctor pointed out the blockage which he called the "widow maker." I had not told my husband that term before. Fortunately, our doctor friend was with us, and he pointed out that that blockage had already been bypassed in his last surgery. I was so glad that we caught this issue before he had an inappropriate surgery. He had more testing and discovered that he had a severely prolapsed heart valve. He had surgery for that, along with two more bypasses.

He never gained his energy back fully. He did keep performing when he could, and he kept working on the most recent revision for his ethics textbook that he had written over thirty years before. He started having more and more problems requiring frequent, lengthy hospitalizations. For months, I continued to operate my business on my computer from his bedside. I realized that he would not be able to be alone anymore, so I was able to transfer the ownership of my business to a nonprofit organization, and I just stayed home with him or at his hospital bedside. After one hospital stay, I stopped by a medical supply store on our way home from the hospital and asked him to please stay in the car. He didn't, and he immediately fell and broke his hip. The anesthetic for that

surgery was overwhelming to his kidneys, so he had to start
dialysis immediately.

The grieving process can start early, long before death, even
though you may not notice. During the two years I stayed home
with Jacques, the number of visitors dwindled, so that even
though he was popular and much loved, we had little support.
An old friend of mine, Yvonne, who lived far away and whom I
hadn't seen in years, happened to come to visit me and ended
up staying with me, helping care for him during his last six
months, and Abby, my daughter, visited from out of state about
once a month, which was a godsend.

Six months later, he had become very weak. He was working
on his most recent textbook update, but he had great difficulty
typing, so every evening I would go through his manuscript
and correct all the typing errors. Finally, he completed
the manuscript, and on a beautiful February morning, we
submitted it electronically to his publisher and had a wonderful
talk with his editor, with lots of smiles, laughs, and celebration.
While he was eating lunch after this, he asked me if he was
going to get better. I couldn't lie to him, so I said "No." He was
having great difficulty walking, so I helped him out to the car to
go to dialysis. He sat on the edge of the car seat, looked at me,
and said "Oh, s***." And he was gone. I tried to get him fully
on the seat so he wouldn't fall to the ground, but he slipped
down the side of the seat, wedged between the seat and the
dashboard where I couldn't help him. I called 911, but it was too
late. We had been married twenty-two years.

After he died, I was sure I would be alone for the rest of my
life, and I was terribly depressed. I went back to work, but I did
not socialize, and had an extremely difficult time. A couple of
years later, Liz, a good friend, encouraged me to date. I thought
she was crazy, but I met a wonderful man, Ron, online. We
fell in love, got married, and had an idyllic life, until he started

to have health problems. This time everything was different. We had many friends we saw regularly, and we traveled whenever we could to see the world. We kept coming back to Maui, where he had lived many years ago. He still had friends there we would visit, and I fell in love with the island. As his health deteriorated, we decided to sell our house in California and move to Maui, where he really wanted to spend the rest of his life.

At first, he seemed so much better in Maui, but his health deteriorated, requiring many hospital stays. With him, everything was so different. We were so in tune spiritually. He was a Religious Science minister, and we truly believed in living in the moment. As soon as we moved into our house, we were surrounded by neighbors and new friends as well as old friends, who immediately became our *ohana*, the Hawaiian word for family. Even though we were fully aware of the direction he was heading, we spent our time living in each moment, smiling, laughing, and loving. Though his original health challenge was congestive heart failure, ultimately his kidneys failed, too, and he had to go on dialysis. The atmosphere at the dialysis center was oppressive, and when he was offered the opportunity to do in-home peritoneal dialysis, he took it. Unfortunately, he appeared to be allergic to the solution and suffered many awful side effects. The doctors just kept saying it would get better as it got worse and worse.

Ultimately, he ended up in the hospital for a week with endless diarrhea, which caused him to lose thirty-five pounds in five days. At the end of that week, he asked the hospitalist physician who had been assigned to his care what they were going to do for him. The doctor said he didn't know—that all he could see was that he had diarrhea and none of the treatments they had tried were helping. So, my husband asked what else they were going to do, but the doctor didn't have an answer.

My husband said he was going home. The doctor said he would have to sign out against medical advice and sent him home without medication which he desperately needed. Fortunately, we had a good friend, Robin, who was a hospice nurse, who made all the arrangements for us and found round-the-clock caretakers and a doctor who would come to the house for the prescriptions he needed. Within a couple of days, he knew he wouldn't get better, so he asked me to set him up with hospice, and we called all of his friends and family.

His last week was amazing; his daughter and his friends from the mainland came and stayed with us. His local friends all came. He was able to FaceTime on his phone with every person in his life who couldn't come, so he could say goodbye. It was a party all week with people singing, listening to music, barbecuing, and sharing so much love. I was with him as he took his last breath.

The experience was so different this time. I was surrounded by love, and I knew I would survive this. I dealt with my loss so differently than I had before. I read everything I could find on grieving, and I started being creative again with my ceramics and sewing. I found people to teach about plant-based cooking. I started writing, mostly journaling, and I found that actually getting things down on paper allowed me to see what I was thinking and experiencing, and this helped me to deal with these experiences.

I ultimately started to breathe again. New truths started emerging, and I discovered new layers of my love and experience. At the end of the first year after Ron died, people were telling me that they could see how much better I was doing, and they were happy for me. Having taught university writing courses for years, I began teaching classes at my home on writing to find joy, which has helped many people through the process of loss. Ultimately, I opened my heart to start reclaiming joy again. And I realized that I really do feel better and life is good!

Why I Wrote This Book

Through my many experiences of loss and learning how to fully live again, I knew that there had to be a way that I could help, love, share with, and support others who are going through similar experiences and are seeking a helpful resource. I finally realized that writing this book would be the best way to help many more people to ease their sorrow and lighten the journey that we all have to make.

This book is an expression of the journey of starting the process of feeling alive again by taking steps to open a new gateway to new living and loving. I wrote this book to encourage you to embrace the process of learning how to start living again and welcoming sustained moments of joy while knowing that you are loved and supported.

I am here for you and the whole tribe of others around the world who find themselves in a place of sorrow, a place that no one asks for, or wants to be in. By approaching this process with an open heart and open arms, we can all learn, love, share, and be the best that we can be. My goal with this book is to meet you where you are and support you on your journey, knowing that everything can only get better from here. Reading the stories in this book and doing the practices that most resonate for you will enable you to be supported as you actively seek a new way of being in the world.

How This Book Can Help You

This is a handbook, akin to the manual in your car's glove compartment, where you pick and choose a topic from the table of contents pertaining to an issue that most needs your attention to solve. Perhaps you are discovering this book in the first year of loss, and you are now actively seeking ways to begin to engage with life again. Or perhaps it's been a few years since your loss, but you're finding the need to be part of a caring community with others who understand what you have been through. Or perhaps your loss is more recent, and you want to learn about specific ways to start engaging with life sooner. Whatever your circumstance, this book is here to offer you a resourceful support. It can help you pull yourself up in a positive way, using the helpful practices and stories to foster joy in living again.

How to Use This Book

This handbook includes twenty-six chapters, each of which contain suggestions for practical actions, which you can download at the end of each chapter and use to reclaim your joy. Each chapter also includes stories from my personal experience and the experiences of others in my extended community who have also experienced loss and found a way to reclaim their joy. I included these stories not only to help ease your journey, but also to help you move through the feelings of isolation and loneliness. These relatable stories will help you to know that others who have been where you are now were able to come out on the other side feeling renewed.

It is important to keep in mind that you are in the driver's seat and can personally direct your progress in choosing how to use this handbook in the best way to serve you in experiencing

the most comfort and strength. You may choose to review the
table of contents and choose a particular chapter and practice
that calls to you. Or you may choose to follow each chapter and
practice sequentially, week by week, for twenty-six weeks and
receive support for six months. Alternatively, you may choose
to read and follow the chapters daily, or only use some of the
suggested practices. However you choose to engage with this
book is up to you, and it's okay. I included more tips at the
end of this chapter for further guidance on how best to use
this book.

Perhaps you may even want to incorporate the suggested
practices into your own daily practices. For example, before
my husband Ron and I moved to Maui, we started each day
by reading something inspirational, meditating, and praying
together. Continuing this practice on Maui, we invited our new
ohana to join us. This daily practice grounded us so that we
started each day in such a positive way. In addition to this, I
developed my own daily practice, which I still use today, that
gives me strength and brings me joy every day.

I suggest taking your time as you move through this book.
There are various practices, some of which may be familiar
to you and some which may be all together new, such as
journaling, practicing gratitude, meditation, prayer, setting
intentions, saying affirmations, and more. Feel free to try
everything and use what works best for you.

Throughout the process, you will discover that there is no
"one-size-fits-all" timeline for experiencing loss. The important
thing is to remember that you are whole, complete, and perfect.
You will discover that the process of using these practices will
help you find peace, comfort, and love.

There is a song, considered a Black American Freedom
spiritual, that was sung frequently during the Civil Rights
movement. I was introduced to it at the Soul Sisters Women's

Retreat, where Mama Byars and Lissa Spinkles would sing it holding hands every year. Reflecting on their strength, love, and joy as they sang this song is a great reminder that you don't have to be alone.

> "Hold my hand while I run this race.
> Hold my hand while I run this race.
> Hold my hand while I run this race.
> Cause I don't want to run this race in vain."
> **—Dr. Claude Joseph Johnson**

I am here for you to hold your hand. My fervent wish is that you find love, support, joy, peace, inspiration, comfort, and the desire to savor each moment for the rest of your life. It's time to get started.

I would love to hear from you while you are on this journey.

Five Tips on Using This Book

1. Take your time reading the book. Pace yourself by not reading more than one chapter at a time.

2. Use a highlighter when you read. Mark what you want to remember or come back to later.

3. Do the practices at the end of each chapter that most resonate for you. In fact, you may want to do each item once, or do each item every day for the week you are reading the chapter.

4. Create your own notebook to use to do the exercises from this book.

5. Take care of yourself while you use this book. Consider the way you use this book a way of giving yourself loving support.

Chapter 1

Lori's Letter

"Try to be a rainbow in someone's cloud."
—Maya Angelou

My husband had a close friend who was about twenty years younger. His name was Chappy, and he called my husband "Dad." We spent lots of time with Chappy and his wife Lori. A few months after my husband died, Chappy died with no warning. I immediately thought of his wife and wanted to help. Since she lived on the mainland and I lived in Hawaii, I couldn't visit or take her a casserole, but I was inspired to write her a letter. The words just flowed from my heart about what she needed to know right then and how she could take care of herself. Knowing that the mail can be very slow from the islands to the mainland, I emailed the letter to Rose, my good friend who lived a couple of blocks from Lori, and asked her to hand-deliver it so she could have it right away.

This is Lori's letter.

My Dearest Lori,

With my words, I send my love to wrap you up and comfort you. There is no easy way to go through the experiences you are having now. The most important thing to remember is that this is the worst that you can feel, and because of that, every moment, every day will be better than the day before. It might not seem like it right now because the better part is so small, but it grows as time passes.

Right now, take care of you. Don't think of it as selfish, but rather, know it is self-care. Cry when you want, be alone when you want, be only with who you want to be when you want, eat what you want, and don't judge yourself for anything. Don't be surprised by anything. If someone says or does something that makes you upset, step back and let that go. People don't know what to say in this situation, and they frequently say strange things, or things that just seem wrong. Don't waste your energy trying to figure out why they say something or do something, just love them. Forgive them. They are trying to do something, but they don't know how.

Let people do things for you. Let them take care of you. If they keep asking what they can do, just ask them to hold your hand and sit with you or get you a cup of tea. You don't need to take care of them right now.

People say some dumb things. Sometimes I feel like if one more person says, "I am sorry for your loss," I will just scream. So now, when someone says that, I think about what could they say that would be better? I know I will never say that, and I know that it is never spoken with malice. I just say thank you.

Saying thank you is healing. I kept track of everything people did and every flower they sent and wrote personal thank-you notes. Something about the process of writing the notes helped me get stronger, helped me to be able to smile again when I did not think that would happen.

I also got a journal just for letters to Ron. I write him whatever I need to, whenever I need to. I can miss him, I can crave him, I can be really angry at him. It doesn't matter. What does matter is that I am expressing how I feel at that moment. And everything I feel, and that you feel, is okay. The more I write about something, the less it weighs on me. Keeping things inside just causes stress and all that comes along with that. Expressing myself is like letting go of a deep breath of air. There are lots of things now that I don't have to keep writing about, and that feels really good.

I also have established a daily meditation practice. It takes different forms all the time. Sometimes it's a walk, sometimes it's sitting outside where it is beautiful. Sometimes it is just being still. This allows me to reboot and refresh. I highly recommend it.

And your dear daughters. Just love them. Listen to them without judgment. They may say some strange things, and that's okay. Just love them. If you can, spend some time sitting with them. They may be really angry in addition to being really sad. And they have a right to be. No one wants to never be able to be with their father again. Just love them. Hold them. Let them know you hear them.

I am always here for you. I have had way too much experience with this, and I would love to use that experience to help you in any way I can.

My love always,

Emily

I kept thinking about Lori and wanted to do more. I knew that one of my biggest challenges after both my husbands died was that many of my friends kind of faded away, especially the first time. One of my creative projects was to make note cards using pictures I take around the island of Maui. I decided that I would send Lori a different card every week. So, I started writing down what I wanted to tell her every week for the first year of her life after Chappy died. I was amazed that the notes just started flowing, and within two days, I had written the content for fifty-two cards, one for each week for a year. The writing process turned out to be therapeutic for me, and I hoped the notes would be therapeutic for her too. And I know that, for this year, each week, she will be reminded that she is loved and supported.

Since Ron died, and I am retired now, I had been trying to figure out what I am supposed to be doing. I had told my granddaughter Katie about the fifty-two cards I wrote, and she called to tell me that her dad's best friend had died suddenly in his fifties and that she wanted to send the cards I had created to his widow. While I was working on putting the cards together for her, I turned on a blog cast on my computer by Lisa Jones, the Millionaire Medium. She read the first chapter of a book she had written about the experience she had when her husband died, which is so powerful. I had read her whole book before, and hearing her speak her experience was amazing. And I thought, "I can do that. I can write a book about the fifty-two ideas I came up with." I am grateful for the inspiration, and hope it will bring love, support, joy, and comfort to people dealing with any kind of loss or with just feeling lost. So here it is.

Practice: Writing Yourself a Letter

The process of writing about my experiences and what I have been learning on this journey has helped me more than anything else. When I wrote my letter to Lori, I realized that I wished someone had written something like this to me when Jacques died. Think what you wish someone would tell you. What do you need to hear? What advice would be most helpful?

Your practice for this chapter is to write a letter to yourself, from your perspective now, that you would have loved to receive right when you started dealing with your situation. This is likely to be an emotional experience. You may want to meditate a while before your start. Take your time with this. You don't have to write it all at once. Start with a draft, and go back to it whenever you think of something else you want to say. When you feel your letter is complete, create a final copy of it. You may want to write it out by hand on nice stationery.

Now, when someone you know has a loved one die or needs support, refer back to this letter. You may want to create a copy for your friend, tailoring it to their situation. Then send it with love. This can be the most cherished and useful information they receive. Remember that each person's situation is different, so each person's needs during this transition process will be different, too. Don't judge yourself on what you write to them. Trust your heart to guide your way.

Key Tips for Chapter 1

- Take good care of your precious self.
- Discover your gratitude.
- Establish your practice of dealing with your feelings by writing.

Chapter 2

Wrap Yourself in Love

"Compassion means 'being with.'"

—Mark Nepo

After attending the funeral of a friend of ours who had died suddenly from a heart issue he did not know he had, we were invited to the home of the family. Everyone was shocked and we felt like we wanted to talk. When we arrived at the home, the family explained to us that they were sitting *shiva*, a term I was not familiar with. *Shiva* is a Jewish tradition where the immediate family of the person who died sits and receives visitors for a week after the funeral. This family was Jewish, but they did not follow all the traditions of the faith. Their *shiva* was more just a pleasant gathering where we all spoke of the one who had passed, and there was lots of food! We only stayed for that first day, but the family did indeed sit *shiva* for the week, and people and food kept pouring in.

I have reflected on this experience and think it would be a wonderful practice for anyone who dies. If friends and family could just hang around for a week, that would provide so much comfort. When Jacques died, Yvonne, a friend of mine, was

living with us and helping with his care. She was my main
support and stayed with me for a few months after Jacques
was gone. Only a few people visited until his memorial service,
which was huge. People were standing in the lobby and on the
sidewalk. The service was amazing.

Our good friend, Dr. Mike Huey, flew out from Georgia to
stage a unique rendition of the play *Our Town*, in which Mike
played the stage manager and showcased Jacques's life. The
service was filled with performances and music, absolutely
perfect for Jacques. And I don't remember most of it because I
was in a fog and exhausted.

There was a reception afterward, and, after that, family and
a few friends came back to the house, but during that time,
few people talked to me. Most came up to me and said the
perfunctory "I'm sorry for your loss," but then went on to talk
to others as I sat by myself. I just watched everyone visit and
laugh and have a good time, which of course was what Jacques
would have wanted, but my feeling alone in the world really
started there. Our children, who lived out of town, returned
home, and after the celebration was over, everyone else
just disappeared.

When Ron transitioned, everything was so different. I had
had a bad fall a few days prior and had refused to go for a
medical evaluation because I couldn't leave Ron at that point.
So Robin made arrangements for me to be seen by a nurse
practitioner the day after Ron transitioned, even though it was
a Saturday. It turned out that I was only bruised, but I did have
a urinary tract infection, which I am sure that I got in part from
not drinking water or paying attention to myself that last week.
That infection made me realize that now it was time for me to
take care of me.

Since close friends and family had gathered with us in Maui
for his last week, they decided we would all go on a dinner

cruise the next night. They shepherded me along and made
sure I was included in everything. Though I didn't feel like
talking, they made sure someone was always sitting with me.
Then, the next night, our friends were playing in a band we
enjoyed, so they all took me there. At one point, when they did
one of Ron's favorite songs, I silently closed my eyes and wept.
When the song was over, I found that my musician friends, as
well as those who had brought me, had gathered around me,
and were holding me in a circle of love.

By the next day, everyone had gone their separate ways, and
I was alone. I found I had no desire to get out of bed, to eat,
to talk to anyone, or to just plain open my eyes. And that was
okay. I felt blank. Shena, who lives in the *ohana* (cottage) on
our property, got to work putting together an ash-scattering
service. I was amazed at the beauty of the traditional Hawaiian
service on the beach. Kimokea, the facilitator, was the husband
of Ren, a special woman who had taken care of Ron that
last week. He did Hawaiian chants and ceremonies, and our
friends spoke of Ron, sang, and did spoken word. Beyond our
close friends, our doctor, our gardeners, our housekeepers,
our insurance agent, and our neighbors were all there. Many
brought beautiful tropical flowers from their yards. Then we got
into outrigger canoes and paddled out into the ocean. Kit went
out on a surfboard to help pass the ashes between the canoes.
We all scattered ashes and flowers. This beautiful ceremony
brought us all so much peace.

Because Ron was a Religious Science minister, he also
wanted to have a service in Los Angeles, at Agape International
Spiritual Center, where his friend Michael Bernard Beckwith
could facilitate. At the airport in Maui, they were remodeling,
and I tripped on the uneven floor, which wasn't barricaded.
I fell hard on the concrete flooring on the opposite hip from
the one I had injured in the last fall. I almost missed my flight

and spent all my time in LA in bed in my hotel room when I wasn't at the service. We had a beautiful service there—our stepson Stephen played bassoon and his wife Jennifer played piano, Rickie Byars sang, Rev. Greta Sesheta and Rev. Deborah Johnson spoke, Michael Bernard Beckwith facilitated, and Ron's daughter Saffronia put together a beautiful video of his life. Our friends had a chance to share their memories. Then we had fabulous vegetarian food by Gwen Kenneally. This time I was more awake and able to actually talk to those who came, and I remember the service.

Having two painful falls so close together showed me that now was the time to take care of me. I was so used to putting everything into Ron's care that I really wasn't taking care of me. I had heard that the death of a spouse is the number-one stressor in life, so—especially since this was my second time around—I knew I had to be awake. I spoke to Cathy, a widow who had always been a bubbly, happy cheerleader-type person. She was always first in line to help others, and everyone was her friend. When her husband died, she said she felt like she had been stuck with a pin, as if she were a balloon, and all the air had come out. She didn't feel like a cheerleader anymore. Her description reminded me that I had discovered that the first thing I needed to do was breathe. Now, I know everyone breathes, but when in deep grief, we sometimes forget. It becomes a labor, or we hold our breath without even realizing that's what we are doing. The first thing to do when you feel overwhelmed, or when the sobbing starts, or when panic arises, is to pay attention to your breath. Try closing your eyes and slowly bringing in air to fill your chest and your abdomen, then letting it out slowly through your mouth. Do that until you start to feel a sense of calm. Breathe like this whenever your emotions start to run amuck. This will bring you peace.

So, right now, wrap yourself up in all that love you have experienced recently, and find comfort in those memories. You are whole, complete, and perfect, and you can get through this time in your life. Just take it one moment at a time.

Practice: Journaling

A journal is a very private item, just for you. You can pour your deepest thoughts and feelings into your journal, and you don't have to share it with anyone. Your feelings right now may range from very sad thoughts, to relief, to gratitude. No one can tell you what to feel right now, and no one can judge you for your feelings. So, express yourself here. Pour your heart out. Say what you need to say. You may have someone right now that you need to talk to about something important, but you just don't know what to say. Practice in your journal. When you start writing freely, you will be amazed at what comes out. If you don't know how to start, just get a pen and your journal and start writing. I promise you, words will come out.

I write in a blank journal. I have filled up a great variety of them over the years, from little blank books I buy, to composition books, to spiral notebooks, to three-ring binders. You can get something like that, or you can write on a new file you set up in your computer. The key is to find what works best for you. I find that, with all the work I do on my computer, I prefer doing my journaling by hand.

For this practice, record what happened when your loved one actually transitioned or when you first started dealing with the issue you are healing from now. This may bring tears, and that's okay. Remembering everything that happened in detail will help you to not have to dwell there. Express it. Write it down. Then move on to your joy. You may want to come back to this entry sometimes, and that's okay. Just write. Don't judge what you are saying, what you did, or what happened. Just report what happened. Writing this way can provide catharsis.

Key Tips for Chapter 2

- Reflect on how you have celebrated the life of your loved one.

- Reflect on who is with you on this journey.

- Remember to breathe when you feel overwhelmed.

Chapter 3

Feeling How You Feel

"Feelings are the language of the soul."

—Annie Sims

There is no right or wrong way to feel. No one can tell you how to feel. Cry when you need to. Laugh when you need to. Just feel what you need to feel in the moment.

When my husband died, I felt like I couldn't feel anything. I didn't want to talk to anyone. I didn't want to do anything. I spent my time in and out of bed based on how my body felt at the moment. Making my bed was not an option because I was likely to get right back into it. I didn't open the shades because the light just seemed to hurt. When Yvonne came home from work, she would make something to eat. She made simple food. Though it tasted fine, the effort to actually eat it was almost overwhelming. I would try. Sort of. But my heart wasn't in it. I started losing weight, and I needed to, so I convinced myself I could get by on very little. However, that resulted in very little energy, which led to more sitting and doing nothing.

I discovered that others have similar feelings. Cherise said she ended up with pneumonia that took weeks to recover from.

She would forget to eat during the day then eat lots late at night. Karen said that things did not go smoothly in the first weeks; there was so much to do and she felt there was a hole in her heart. And Jean said she had grief piling up, making it difficult to deal with life. Knowing that helped; though it seemed so, I really was not alone.

A friend of mine, Guinevere, had created a program that provided acting classes for children. I have always supported arts opportunities for children, especially since the public-school system cut back on most of these classes. She was having a fundraiser, selling things to support the classes, and I had lots of leftover yarn and plenty of crochet hooks and patterns, so I started crocheting away, making scarves. I even got creative by putting beads in the fringes, and I made so many, I even started buying yarn. I didn't even have to leave the house. But then the fundraiser was over, and I almost felt loss for not having crocheting to do, so I figured it was time for me to find a way to make good use of my time.

When Jacques died, the kids had moved away, and I was left in a big four-bedroom home with terrifying drug- and alcohol-using neighbors. Yvonne, who had been staying with me to help care for Jacques, was moving back home to Alaska, so my next project was finding a place to live. House-hunting took up most of my time. I made lists of everything I'd love to have, what location was right for me, and what I would be comfortable paying, Ultimately, we came up with the perfect place for me to live alone, a large two-bedroom, two-bathroom house in a small planned unit development that was fenced, so I felt safe. The whole process of moving and decorating helped give me something positive to do and helped to bring me back into the world of others.

Meanwhile, the university called and said they would really like to have me come back to teach. Not only that, but I could combine my new teaching contracts with my old ones to lead to retirement. I was thrilled with this opportunity.

Through all this adventure, I still was not connecting much with people. I knew I needed to, but making the first move has always been challenging for me. It really hit me when I was sitting at home, alone, on New Year's Eve, with no plans for the night or for the new year. I knew I had to start somewhere. I hadn't learned anything about meditation yet, but I figured I would try. I sat for hours with soft baroque music playing in the background and tried clearing my thoughts, knowing the answer would come. Then it did. I knew that I had to accept invitations. This sounded so bizarre to me. In all the time that I had been alone, the invitations hadn't exactly started rolling in. I thought of myself as the black widow that everyone was afraid to get near. Of course, now I know that was just a roadblock I had built for myself, but it was very effective at the time. So, what invitations, exactly, was I supposed to accept? I didn't know. I just decided to say "Yes!"

I was reading the local newspaper one day and the first invitation jumped out at me. They were looking for new members to appoint to the editorial board. I knew nothing about doing something like this, but I did like reading the newspaper, and I always seemed to have an opinion, so I applied for the position and got it. Then I was asked to be on the board for my planned unit development. And I was asked to be the nurse for an ultramarathon bicycle racing team. And I was asked to create a film festival for the County Board of Trade. And I was asked to take my late husband's position on the ethics committee of the local hospital. And I decided to go on a vacation to explore Puerto Rico, where my son-in-law was from. And I did it all!

Whew! What a year that was. I had not planned to be a widow. I had not planned to be alone. And I certainly had not planned to participate in all these new activities. I wasn't dating or meeting new friends, but I was learning how to talk again, learning how to breathe. I am grateful for the variety of activities and variety of people I met in the process. I became comfortable having conversations and getting out of my house. I realized that I was not doomed to be alone forever, which was an overwhelming feeling that would come up in those first few months. I learned that I could take care of myself, and to keep my eyes, and ears, and heart open for the next step. And that the next step didn't have to be from one marriage into another just because that was where I was comfortable in the past. I learned that I was okay, and you are too. Your experience will be different from anything you have dreamed of, and you can do this!

Practice: Prayer

You may already have your own practice with prayer. If you do, keep doing what works for you. If you don't have your own prayer practice, or if you don't believe in prayer, or religion, or God, please don't skip this tool. You can send your prayer out into the universe, knowing that expressing yourself this way will bring you much. You can pray anywhere and to anyone. You may pray to God, to the Source of Everything, to Buddha, or to Jesus. Who you pray to doesn't matter. What matters is that you take the time to sit still and be with the source of everything good. Express your gratitude. Express your love. Or just sit quietly in silence, if that is what works for you right now. Do this every morning when you wake up. And do it again whenever you feel inspired.

When you pray, find a quiet place where you will not be disturbed. You may do this out loud or silently, whichever works best for you. Start by expressing gratitude. You can't express too much gratitude! Next, send love and support to all those who need it. You don't need to be specific. For instance, if you have a friend who is dealing with cancer, instead of asking for the cancer to be cured, you can send love and support to this person, asking for what is highest and best in this circumstance. My Ron always used to say not to pray for body parts or illness, but to pray for comfort and love. What you speak will come to you, and I would rather have comfort and love come than have illness come. Know that what you say in prayer is your truth, and speak whatever you say as if it is already done by saying something like, "I speak this word of truth, knowing that what I say here, I know, is already done." After you say your prayer, release it into the universe. Try doing this at least once a day.

Key Tips for Chapter 3

- Feel what you need to in the moment.
- Remember to eat and find a way to exercise.
- Consider now what activities you can do to help yourself and others.

Chapter 4

Meditation

"To offer no resistance to life is to be in a state
of grace, ease, and lightness."

—Eckhart Tolle

Practicing meditation can bring you peace. Many people have a regular meditation practice they do every day, sometimes more than once a day. Others say they find it impossible to meditate because they just can't quiet the mind, or what Eckhart Tolle refers to as "the voice in the head." Whatever your situation has been up to now, meditation may be especially challenging, but it can also be extremely healing, so it is worth doing. Researchers have discovered that meditation can actually change your neurochemistry, meaning it physically helps you.

Meditation will not take pain away, but it will help you cultivate compassion for yourself. One of the ways meditation can help you is to break the cycle of thoughts that run through your mind. Often, when trying to fall asleep, I would get stuck on certain moments of my husband's care, like whether the decisions we made were the best ones for him. Though I realized I couldn't go back to change anything, I would think about how, if only we had made different decisions, maybe the outcome would have been different. Self-talk like this can escalate and make it difficult to fall asleep. I discovered that, when I intentionally meditated at bedtime, I could clear those thoughts and get to sleep.

Other symptoms you may have to deal with are muscle pain from tightness or headaches. You may know that if you relax you will feel better, but just telling yourself to relax is likely to create more tension and more discomfort. And this can occur when you are at work or in the middle of doing something that you can't take a break from. I have several meditation apps on my phone and even have a variety of meditation music stations on Pandora and Amazon Music. When I can't get away to meditate, I put on one of these apps or stations. If I am not alone, I put on my earphones, and the music and sounds, along with slowing my breath, will help me focus on what I am doing and release the tension which is likely to have caused the discomfort.

Loss can also affect your immune system, and meditation can give it a boost by allowing you to relax and take care of yourself. There is a big difference between lying in bed because you are too sad to get up and lying down to actively meditate, when you relax and release the tension that your feelings are hammering you with. Use your meditation to create a barrier for yourself against stress and trauma. Establishing a strong meditation practice will help you not only now, but for the rest of your life. Make meditation a regular practice.

When I first started to meditate, I did a form of mindfulness meditation where I would focus on my breath and use a word that was meaningful to me at the time on my inhale and exhale. For instance, I would breathe in thinking, "unconditional love," and breathe out thinking, "peace." I would use whatever words were meaningful to me at the moment. After doing that for a while, I would soften my closed eyes and focus on the area of my forehead, just peacefully breathing until I felt complete. At other times, I would do a body scan meditation, focusing on relaxation. I would get in a comfortable position and take several long, deep, cleansing breaths. Then I'd start relaxing every part of my body, one part at a time, starting with my toes. I'd feel each muscle relax and discover the energy coursing through the spaces between my cells. When I completely relaxed, I felt light, almost floating, and was able to maintain this peaceful state, focusing on breathing.

Another form of meditation I do is something Ron taught me long ago. I was having a particularly stressful day. He was driving us someplace, and he pulled into a parking lot and told me to close my eyes. He took me through slow, deep breathing to get started, and when I had calmed down, he guided me to create the most peaceful place I could think of. I went to a memory from my childhood of a clearing in the mountains, with the clean scent of pine in the air. I sat in a most comfortable place, and he asked me who was there with me. I felt the presence of a little sprite flying around and taking care of me, and at the moment I really wanted to be taken care of. He asked me if I had a wisdom source there, and I did, and a source of strength, and I did. And the three of them had names. By the time we finished it all, I felt so much better. The amazing thing about this meditation to me is that I still go to that exact space, with those three beings, with the same names I have remembered all these years. I go there often, and they still care for me and provide strength and wisdom, and they have been joined now by my spirit guides and angels. I encourage you to find your very special place, to go to and return there whenever it serves you. This is a wonderful place to deal with the sorrow, a place where you are always fully supported and loved.

We all experience stress and loss at various times in our lives. This can come from the ending of relationships, the end of a career, the loss of a home, or from the losses caused by natural disasters. We think of grief most frequently in terms of the loss of life, whether it be of a spouse, a friend, a relative, a partner, or a pet. And we all deal with our feelings in different ways. The self-care of a meditation practice can be most comforting and healing, and I strongly encourage you to establish your own practice if you haven't already. Being present with your feelings and being mindful of what you learn through loss can be accomplished with meditation and can bring you peace and decrease any depression or anxiety.

Our culture wants us to be strong and overcome our feelings. When I hear people say things like this, I assume they have not been close to someone who has died. But I have learned to not judge people because we are each on our own path. By eliminating judgment from my life, I have allowed myself to be more vulnerable. I can feel, see, and share my darkest moments, or not. I can just be mindful of my experiences along the way and know that I am okay. I am just going through experiences all of us do in life. I always remember both of my husbands who died, and I will always love them dearly. That does not cut me off from being able to love anyone else. What it does is allow me to know that I love deeply, unconditionally, always.

Many people deal with stress and loss by trying to block it, by getting so busy with work or activities that they don't take time to deal with it. This method just delays healing. Meditation is a wonderful way to deal with your feelings by allowing yourself to sink into what you are experiencing, become one with it, and move into a place of peace. When I meditate, I feel the feelings I am experiencing right now. You can find power from intentionally being still and feeling what you feel. Remember the wonder and beauty of your life instead of dwelling on the time you don't have. Your love will always survive.

If you regularly meditate, please continue your practice. You may want to increase the frequency or length of your meditation, or you may want to try different methods. When you meditate, be sure to find a place where you will not be interrupted and where you can be comfortable. Be sure the temperature is comfortable for you. You may want to create a special place in your home, like an altar, where you can place items that bring you comfort. These items could be candles, incense, flowers, crystals, pictures of your loved one, a beautiful fabric, an icon like a Buddha or a tribal amulet, special stones, or any items which bring you peace. You also may want to freshen or rearrange your meditation space on a regular basis.

If you don't have a regular meditation practice, this is the perfect time to start. I practice a variety of ways to meditate. Besides the ones I have already mentioned, sometimes I want some help, so I will go to meditation apps on my phone or videos on YouTube. The quality varies widely, but having choices makes learning to meditate an ongoing experience for me.

I took *qi gong* classes which ended each session with a crystal bowl meditation, and I discovered that the sound and vibration from the bowls allowed me to get into a deeper state than I have been on my own. You can find crystal bowl meditations online or on something like Pandora.

I went to a women's retreat, Soul Sisters, that had optional healing sessions, and I decided to go for a sound healing. The setting was outside at a lovely gazebo with light, gauzy curtains gently moving with the breeze. The practitioner led me to a massage table draped with lovely fabrics and had me lie on my back. He put a soft pillow over my eyes. For the next hour,

I felt transformed to a different dimension. He used a variety of instruments, from singing bowls to rattles, to gongs, to rain sticks, and I don't know what else. Up to this point, I had never experienced a deeper meditation. This was my introduction to sound healing, and I became a firm believer. All outside distractions were eliminated, and all the sounds permeated my body and felt like they were communing with my soul.

Now I have discovered sound baths. Sound baths take all the elements of sound healing and magnify them. Though usually done in a group setting, you can find people who will offer a private sound bath. A sound bath may start with a sitting guided meditation, leading to a break where participants lie down on the floor on yoga mats and support themselves with pillows for comfort. The room is filled with instruments which vary depending on who is playing them. The instruments can be Himalayan singing bowls, crystal bowls, gongs, biosonic tuning forks, crystal harps, shamanic drums, and more. Sometimes singing or chanting is also done, usually without words. As you relax with your eyes closed, the music starts and washes over you and through the room. The deep gongs can feel like they are penetrating right through you. The sound is so encompassing that thoughts dissolve and pure, deep meditation settles in. You don't have to listen as the music surrounds you. Just feel soft and enjoy the process. If you haven't experienced a sound bath yet, please do.

When you are ready to meditate, check your surroundings. Remove anything distracting. Be sure the temperature is appropriate for relaxation. If you desire, have soothing music, preferably without words so your monkey mind won't sing along. When you start to meditate, focus on your heart center. Feel any pain you are experiencing, let it soften, then release that pain. Release any emotions that do not serve you, like anger, sadness, or unanswered questions. Recognize that you have all the strength you need within you. And recognize that, though it may not seem like it sometimes, you are always deeply loved and are never alone.

With any meditation practice, plan it so that you don't have to rush back to anything. Take time for yourself afterward. Have a cup of tea, take a walk, take a bath, take a nap, or go to bed. Journaling is also a wonderful practice after meditation. I often come out of meditation with profound inspiration that I don't want to forget. And what I write in my journal can also help inspire me the next time I meditate. Meditation is a perfect practice of self-care.

Practice: Meditation

If you already have your own meditation practice, just keep doing what you are doing. If practicing meditation is new for you, that's okay. Just commit to trying the concept of being still and clearing your mind. You can do it anytime, anyplace, alone, or with anyone you choose. Just be open. I recommend meditating at least once a day for at least ten minutes at a time.

If you haven't meditated, you can start by finding a quiet place where you will not be disturbed. I have a platform/ treehouse in a giant avocado tree in my yard that is so peaceful to me. Find a place that works for you. You may have a spot in your home that works, where you can keep a few things that bring you peace, like crystals, candles, little statues, pictures, incense, or whatever you are most comfortable with. Go to this place. Sit up with a straight back and open hands. Set a timer for ten minutes. And start by breathing and concentrating on your breath as it flows in and flows out. Close your eyes. Just be still and breathe. When the timer goes off, open your eyes, take a deep breath, and smile. See how easy that was!

Key Tips for Chapter 4

- Practice a form of meditation daily.

- Examine any physical symptoms you are currently experiencing and develop a plan to deal with them.

- Be present with your feelings and be mindful of what you learn.

Chapter 5

Cocooning

"Pain is inevitable. Suffering is optional."

—Michael Bernard Beckwith

Cocooning is a time when all you can do is maybe sit at home in front of a fire, and that is okay. If you don't want to go somewhere, don't. Be easy on yourself now, because your feelings at this time can be unpredictable.

A few months before Ron transitioned, we were sitting on our *lanai*, Hawaiian for deck, in our beautiful backyard. We lived on the side of Haleakala, a dormant volcano, that gently sloped down our yard vibrant with avocado, Ficus, banana, and papaya trees and much tropical foliage, including giant hibiscus and lilikoi plants. We frequently witnessed rainbows from this perch which appeared to be lower than we were, allowing us to think that we lived romantically over the rainbow. Enjoying the gentle trade winds, yellow and black butterflies were plentiful, and would actually land on Ron as though they were attracted to him. He told me that there would come a time when, every time I saw a butterfly or a rainbow or smelled the smoke

of a cigar, which he relished every day, I would know that
he was near.

A few months after he was gone, I was feeling in a vacuum
where time seemed to be standing still, and I couldn't connect
with the world. Before I started being with Ron constantly
because of his health, I loved doing ceramics. When we moved
to Maui, he had a perfect studio built for me in our yard, but
I couldn't seem to go there to create. I felt blank. I decided I
had to do something, so I signed up for a ceramics class at the
Hui No'eau Visual Arts Center in Makawao. The translation of
hui no'eau is "people coming together for a common purpose
for the development of artistic skill and the wisdom which
derives from that expression." This sounded to me like the
perfect place to open my path to healing. When driving to class,
I was surrounded by butterflies. I have never seen so many
butterflies in the same place. They floated around my car for
literally miles, and, unlike before, when I have had butterflies
or moths come to their ends against my car window or grille,
not one stuck to the car. And of course, that week there were
rainbows too.

This experience made me realize that I was cocooning. We
have a big Brugmansia plant in our yard which the common
name for is angel's trumpet. I had noticed that it had been
covered with caterpillars that were yellow and black. I found it
ironic that the butterflies, which were also in my yard, had been
created from the caterpillars eating the angel's trumpet vines.
I looked this process up, and it was different from what I had
been told in school years ago. What really happens is that the
caterpillar sheds its skin and a protective shell called a chrysalis
is formed. Then everything inside the chrysalis turns into a
liquid that is similar to human stem cells. From this comes
what are called imaginal cells, which sounds to me like the
imagination where new things come from. Though there is no

structural similarity between the caterpillar and the butterfly, these cells transform into beautiful butterflies.

I remember that, in one of Ron's sermons, he told the story of a person who noticed a chrysalis moving. That person assumed the butterfly was working to emerge, so he decided to help. But the process of breaking out of the chrysalis is crucial to building the strength of the butterfly so it can survive, and by the person helping this process along, the butterfly that emerged died. This made me think of the process I was experiencing.

For several months after Ron's transition, I felt like that goo that forms during the transformation from the caterpillar to the butterfly. I felt like it was too hard to think, to eat, to walk, to read, or really to do anything. During this time, I recorded and watched many silly romantic movies I didn't have to think about. The plots were formulaic, and there was always a happy ending. The movies were actually just background noise. If I stayed in silence or tried to listen to music, my monkey mind would run wild. The movies dulled the pain. I could lie in bed and actually feel like I was being held. I see now that was like my own chrysalis, and that I had to go through this process to help me adjust or transition to my new life.

Everybody will experience this process in their own way. This is the time where you prepare for or develop the skills that will help you move forward. For some, this gestation is relatively brief. Others take a long time. The key is to recognize that this is normal and to do what you need to so that you can take care of yourself. I would sit on my lanai or soak in my bathtub without putting any restrictions on myself. This may be a time where you resist the change that you have been forced into. Everything can't help but be different without your loved one in your life. This was not something you can plan for or escape. Releasing into the process will ultimately help bring

you peace and allow your butterfly to emerge. This is the time
when your transformation occurs.

You will think new thoughts and do things differently than
you ever have before. Know that this is okay. As much as you
would like to go on the way things were before, you can't.
Take this time to explore what to do now, and be patient with
yourself. This isn't a time for a quick fix or a magical solution.
Your feelings do not disappear, but you will become used to
them. You will assimilate it into your life so that it changes
from being all-encompassing to being a natural part of you.
As you shed your old skin, you can shed your old habits that
no longer serve you. You can grow and develop your new,
beautiful, powerful wings.

Many refer to loss or death as a transition, but you are
going through a transition, too, and it may feel like you are
dying. Actually, the old you is dying. The new you will have
different hopes and dreams and desires. You may have a
tendency to fight this transition as you would fight death if
you are not ready, but that will only prolong the process. The
most important part of the journey Ron and I shared was to
commit to living in the moment. We dealt with any symptom
that came up when it came up. We did not worry in advance
about what would be happening next. And actually, I didn't
realize that he was really dying. Our moments were so precious,
sharing our love, having long wonderful talks or just sitting in
silence enjoying the beauty of our surroundings. His birthday
was about a month before he left, and Shena gave him the book
Death of a King, by Tavis Smiley, which was the story of Martin
Luther King's last year. He wanted to read it, but he discovered
that reading was difficult for him, so I read the entire book to
him out loud. Those are cherished moments. Time stood still
as we were immersed in the greatness of this man. Having
this experience helped me stay in the moment as I was going

through this cocooning process. All I dealt with was how I was feeling or what was happening to me at that time, right then. And living in the moment has allowed me to move forward one moment at a time.

Right now, think about what you can do that feels best. You may like to have a cup of tea, go for a walk, read a book, or record and watch silly romance movies. Whatever it is, do it. Don't judge yourself or your desires. I found myself putting together puzzles or playing Sudoku. The process of keeping occupied allowed me to not just sit and cry, although there is nothing wrong with that. Tears are cleansing, and I have certainly cried until my eyes feel dry. The key is not living in fear, which is the opposite of love. Right now, love yourself. Fearing being alone or fearing your future does not serve you. Loving yourself unconditionally will always serve you.

This is the time to seek out a friend who has been through this process. Your friend may have experienced a different kind of loss, but everyone does go through a process of some form of cocooning. What matters is that you can support each other. I noticed that, during this time after the deaths of both my husbands, friends mostly kept their distance. I assume that they didn't know what to say or did not want to be dragged down into my despair. And I didn't seem to be able to reach out to my friends. If the experience is similar for you, this may be the time you'd like to seek counseling. There are many counselors out there who specialize in grief, but I suggest you go to one who has actually experienced loss. The common experience can make all the difference in how helpful a counselor can be.

Cocooning can be so hard on your body and soul. Be aware of this, and take care of yourself during the process. Be sure to rest, to eat, and to exercise. And, in the words of Dr. Alan B. Wolfelt, "Feelings have one ambition, to be felt." So, feel what you feel. Love who you love. Grieve how you grieve. But most of all, be gentle with yourself.

Practice: Journaling

I journal regularly and will give you ideas for what to write about in your journal for several of the chapters. Cocooning reminded me of something I heard Michael Bernard Beckwith say in an interview with Katy Koontz: "Become mindful of the emotions and mindsets that hook you, that trigger you. Ask yourself, 'Am I caught in a societal point of view, such as fear, worry, lack, doubt, or limitation?' Then, instead of denying that negative emotion, observe it and try to embrace it. By being mindful that you are in a state of fear and embracing rather than adopting it, you can examine its underpinnings."

Have you noticed any negative emotions during cocooning? Can you embrace and examine these emotions? Write about this in your journal. If you did not notice these emotions, what emotions did you feel? How have they affected you? Write about this in your journal.

I also encourage you to write in your journal regularly to explore your emotions and express your feelings. Your journal can be like your best friend and confidant.

Key Tips for Chapter 5

- Consider the skills you can learn to move forward.
- Recognize that everything is different now.
- Do what feels best for you right now.

Chapter 6

Loss

*"As long as you are breathing, there is more
right with you than wrong with you."*

—John Kabit-Zinn

Your stress or loss is as bad as you think. Others will want to tell you how to think or do things, and that is not their decision. Things will never be the same, and how you react is up to you. Be easy on yourself, and don't judge yourself or the people who want to help.

With both of my husbands, I knew that the time we had left was limited, and at the same time, I just couldn't imagine life without them. When they transitioned, both times, the cold, hard realization that they were gone hit me like getting a swift, hard kick to my chest. First the air was completely knocked out of me, and when I tried to breathe, all that escaped were sobs that kept getting bigger and bigger. I felt as if I was sealed in a bubble of unreality. For the first few days, I slipped in and out of awareness of what was happening around me. Even when people spoke to me, everything seemed foggy. When I finally broke through, I had an extreme feeling of aloneness.

Stress and loss are painfully real, and each of us will deal in our own way. There is no right way. You don't need instructions. There are many emotions you may deal with. Some of them are yearning, shock, guilt, confusion, worsening of physical problems and pain, anxiety, chronic fatigue, fear, and weight gain or loss. Whew! That's a big list, and I'm sure there are more things you can think of to add. Let's talk about this list.

Yearning: One of my favorite things was to lie with Ron in our bed, spooning. We had agreed that our bedroom was a sacred space, with no television, electronic devices, or reading, unless we were reading to each other. We had created a perfect, peaceful environment for celebrating our love and enjoying what Michael Barnard Beckwith calls Sacred Energy eXchange. Being alone in that perfect bed and room was almost impossible for a while after he was gone. My yearning for his touch, for his breath on my neck, for his arm draped over me as we slept, was unbearable. I took to sleeping, the little I did, on the couch, but there came a point where I could almost hear him say to me, "How does that serve you?" When I considered that, I realized that it didn't serve me at all. My neck and back were sore. I had headaches. I didn't sleep very long at a time. So I went back to bed, and I finally could rest.

Karyn had this experience: "I still feel yearning for Jim sometime of every day, even though he has been gone from me in the body since 2006. I yearn for his stability and loving presence. It was as if he held me in his arms above the everyday sorrows of losing him. For quite a while I felt his spirit with me. Now I know he has gone on. I see him in nature. The yellow swallowtail butterfly that flits through my morning meditations is a good example. I see it daily and I am comforted."

Shock: My phone rang late one night. My mother called to say that they had taken my dad to the hospital. She thought it was his heart, but they told her he was stable, and she should go home and get some rest. I assured her that I would make the hour's drive first thing in the morning to be with them. An hour later, she called, and he had died. We were all in shock. My husband Jacques and I immediately drove to be with her. We all just sat there. We hadn't ever really thought that Dad or Mom might not be with us anymore, though of course we knew it was inevitable. When it came so fast, we were just in shock. That took a while to work through. I would want to call Dad, and I'd realize I couldn't. His empty chair at holidays just didn't seem real. And, though it was shocking at the time, we gradually realized the truth of his departure.

Cathy, a recent widow, told me of the shock of coming home to find her husband on the floor, unable to move. He said he didn't want to go to the hospital to die, so she sat with him all night, and he finally agreed to go. He died several days later. She said that, several months later, the husband of her friend died choking on food, leaving her with two young children. The shock of that helped her with perspective.

Guilt: Guilt can occur when we fret about things that happened that we cannot change. Knowing that there is nothing we can do about this guilt at this point doesn't make it easier, but recognizing what happened and releasing that guilt about it can help.

Marla, a widow of two years, said, "Guilt has plagued me almost incessantly, though less so since seeing a grief counselor about every two weeks over the past two years since my husband died. I feel I could have loved him better and could have/should have prevented my husband's death. Often feeling guilty for being alive intensifies my effort to connect more fully with my family and Gaia."

Karen, a widow of two years, said: "Guilt surfaces for me when I think about my leaving him that last weekend and not being with him at the end; and when I couldn't coax him into talking about his passing. I wish all of that could have gone differently."

Confusion: My mother would forget that my father had died, and when anyone pointed it out to her, she would be so confused, not being able to process what had happened. And she would be confused about things like paying bills or taking care of herself because things just didn't make sense to her anymore. With her, we ultimately discovered that she had a physical condition adding to this confusion. So, realize that confusion frequently happens to people after a loss, but if it doesn't go away, be sure to get it checked out medically.

Worsening of physical problems: If you already have some kind of physical problem going on, don't be surprised if it gets worse, and do let a medical professional help you. Sometimes we give up our will to heal or get better, or our willingness to participate in our own healing. Take some time to really examine what is going on with you and discover what you need to do about it. For example, Lindsey had an ailing husband on his final path, and each time he ended up in the hospital or had a complication, a current physical challenge of hers worsened or a new one came up. We are so in tune with the ones we love that this synchronicity can happen. If this seems to be happening with you, please get it checked out.

Fear: Fear can come from many directions: fear of living alone, fear of new financial challenges, or fear of not knowing what to do. I discovered that I was afraid of my neighbors when Jacques died. Though I had lived next to them for twenty years, their little boys had grown up to follow in the violent footsteps of their alcoholic father. In their eyes, they could do no wrong. The oldest son had a big scar on his face from a knife fight in a bar. As long as Jacques was alive, they left us alone. But that all changed when he died. They did ask me if they could use my swimming pool, and I told them no, so they took that as an invitation to come party in my pool, breaking glass bottles on the concrete deck whenever they wanted to. They would yell vulgar things at me if they saw me outside of the house. I feared they would attack me physically, so I called the police to ask for help, but they just talked to the family, who promised they'd leave me alone—but when the officer left, things just got worse. When I found a used condom in the pool, I decided I had to make a change. I sold my house and moved into a much smaller place that was perfect for just me. That solved my fear problem, but some problems don't have a clear path for change.

The good news is that there is always a way to get help to release that fear. Just don't be afraid to ask for help. If your fear is financial, start with your banker, or ask a trusted friend for guidance. If it is fear of being alone, find people with whom you share common interests. If it is fear of not knowing what to do, really explore what you want to do and try things out, whether it is learning a new skill, getting a new job, or traveling the world. Just try something. Get started. Step out there.

Weight gain or loss: I have seen people gain large amounts of weight after loss by eating unconsciously. The process of putting food in their mouths becomes automatic. They don't seem to taste food or particularly enjoy eating anymore. Eating just becomes an escape. I've seen more people lose weight. Jane, a widow of one year, was shocked that she easily lost weight after trying to lose weight for years with no success. She just ate less when she was alone. Hannah gained weight because, after forgetting to eat during the day, she ate lots at night. I lost weight both times. I no longer was interested in going out to eat. And I wasn't interested in eating much of anything. I discovered that I could live on vegetables, especially asparagus, mashed potatoes, and corn. And the weight just melted away. I was grateful for the weight loss, but there came

a point where I really had to start paying attention to what I
ate. And I do now. The key is to be conscious about what you
eat, and to eat what you know will nourish you.

So now that you have experienced this loss, what can you do
about it? The answer to this question is going to be different for
each person. In listing a few ways here, I hope you'll try some
and see what helps you.

- **Your New Normal:** Everyone has experienced or
  will experience loss in their lives, some lots more than
  others. Grief is normal and is actually an expression
  of love. When you get to the point where you can
  accept this, you can deal positively with what is good
  about your life. One of my favorite essays by Howard
  Thurmond is "I Want to be More Loving in My Life."
  What do you want to be?

- **Talk to Someone:** If you could talk about your
  deepest feelings to someone right now, who would
  that be? Do you have a friend you can talk to, or
  would you rather talk to a stranger, like a counselor?
  Choose someone, and talk to whoever it is. Develop
  a soul-to-soul communication that can serve you
  both. A friend of mine went to a psychic and raved
  about how wonderful she was. I am not sure that I
  believe in psychics, but I decided to take a chance
  and go to her. I really don't remember much of what
  she said, just that she was loving and supportive. I
  ended up pouring things out to her that I hadn't been
  comfortable talking about to people I knew well. I left
  feeling relieved and grateful for the experience. So,
  talking to someone can really help. Just pick someone
  you will be comfortable with.

- **Social Media:** One way to deal with loss that many people turn to nowadays is social media. After I read *Option B* by Sheryl Sandburg, I actually felt much better, and I happened to find a support group on Facebook for people who had read *Option B*. I was thrilled and spent a lot of time going to that group online for a while, until I discovered that so many people were hurting so deeply, and reading about their pain was bringing me more pain. So I decided that I didn't have to continue reading every entry. When I read an entry that I could relate to, I started writing positive things in reply that I hoped would be helpful. I discovered they were helpful, for me. I hope they were helpful for others too. There is something about being surrounded by a tribe of people who are experiencing things you are experiencing or have experienced that makes you feel not quite so alone in the world. I have joined a couple more groups and discovered some work for me, and some don't. Just try.

- **Do Something:** Many of us get into a rut of staying at home and not doing anything. I love to do ceramics and have a studio on my property I love to work in, yet I just couldn't convince myself to go there. I decided I needed to do something entirely different. Shena is on the board for a children's arts education group, and she had been asked to run the silent auction for their fundraiser. She asked me to help, and I said yes. The process of getting ready for the auction took a lot of time and was something I could easily do from home. I relished the opportunity and discovered that, by the time we were ready for the auction, I was ready to attend. Getting out to do something so positive for our community was a huge step forward for me in coming out of my cocoon.

What is something you could do that you would enjoy?

- **Explore Your Spirituality:** If you so believe, you can find comfort in your place of worship, whatever it may be. They may have some form of compassionate meetings to help you. Or maybe they have special books or counseling available.

- **Attend a Support Meeting:** When Ron died, hospice kept inviting me to attend their group meetings, and I just couldn't. I had conjured up a vision of an uncomfortable room where everyone just sat around and cried and felt sorry for themselves. Now, I know that's probably not the case, but just thinking about that made me agitated, and I just couldn't go. Then I heard about different kinds of groups that happen here in Maui. In one of them, people just shared about how life is going on for them after their loss. The atmosphere was comfortable and positive. So I decided to go to the other group that the same people host, a Death Café. I had never heard of such a thing. We gathered at a Mexican restaurant and shared stories of our loved ones and how we felt, and we were able to laugh and share our love over guacamole. I enjoyed it so much that I became the facilitator for the Death Café on Maui. So, try a group. If the first one doesn't work, try again till you find one that suits you.

- **Change What You Can:** When Marla's husband died, her home of many years had just been sold to the city to be demolished to make way for new freeway construction. So she lost her husband and her

home at the same time. With encouragement from
her children, she moved across the country to buy a
home close to them and was able to start a new life
with a big new garden and grandchildren. I went back
to an old career, teaching writing at the university,
when they called and asked me if I was available.
Your changes don't need to be so big. What would
you like to change? You could take a class, paint your
living room, or learn to cook a new cuisine. You could
register people to vote, volunteer at a hospital, or
learn how to garden. Think of things you like, and try
something new.

Loss is hard. We all react differently. From my personal
experience, my mother was disappointed that she didn't die
at the same time Dad did. Mom and Dad always thought they
would die in a car accident, since they traveled so much in
their car. After Dad died, she didn't smile again till she was
diagnosed years later with a terminal illness. For me, about two
years after Jacques died, I had to have surgery. The hospital
I had to go to was undergoing renovations, and the room
they took me into for the pre-op exam was the room where
Jacques had died. My blood pressure was sky-high, and they
almost cancelled the surgery. I thought I was doing well, but
in that circumstance, I wasn't. Don't be surprised, as your life
goes on, when things come up to remind you what you have
been through.

After Jacques died, that first year was the longest year of
my life. Time stood still, and moving forward was harder than
I had ever dreamed. My relationship with Ron was so different.
We consciously lived in each moment. We said everything we
wanted to say and experienced together everything we wanted
to experience. He was ready to go and happy his transition was
coming. This first year after his departure has been the shortest

in my life. And I am grateful. Remember when you start feeling your loss that, ultimately, things will keep getting better.

Practice: Write a Poem about Your Loss

Poems can range from structured, specific rhyming forms to loose free verse and everything in between. For this poem, write something loose and free. Don't constrain yourself with any rules; rather, write from your heart. The subject for this poem is your stress or loss. Write about it. Get it all out. Say everything you need to say. Write for as long as you need to. Allow this to be your catharsis. You may focus on a specific incident, or you may explore your personal loss in general. You could write it like a list of all the things you have lost. Or you could flip from loss to what you have found or discovered in what you are experiencing. Writing a poem instead of a journal entry can free the creative right side of your brain to come up with thoughts that might not have come forward without this freedom. After you write your poem, set it aside for a couple of days, then look at it again. You might come up with more to say or notice things you learned about yourself when you read your poem again.

Key Tips for Chapter 6

- The loss you experienced is real and it is huge.
- Everyone experiences loss in their life, often many times.
- You can move on in life after great loss.

Chapter 7

Gratitude

" 'Thank you' is the best prayer that anyone could say. I say that one a
lot. Thank you expresses extreme gratitude, humility, understanding."

—Alice Walker

When I thought I didn't really have anything to live for, I
started writing down what I am grateful for. I found I kept
writing more things and making new lists, and that I wasn't
repeating myself. This showed me how good my life actually
was and that I really had lots to live for.

For a long time after Jacques died, I didn't smile. Life just
kind of happened, and I just let it. A couple of my friends, Joe
and Ruth, were concerned about me and gave me a copy of
the movie *The Secret* to watch. I watched it with a chip on my
shoulder. I didn't see how anything that it said had anything
to do with me. It seemed like the movie was about magical
thinking, where I could just decide I wanted something, and
I would have it. I didn't see how that could be true. After I
watched the movie, I noticed that, in the case for the DVD,
there was a sheet that said, "Don't turn this over until you've
watched the movie." Since I had watched the movie, I turned

it over, and it was simply a sheet with lines and a statement at the top that said to write down things I was grateful for. My attitude was, *yeah, right*, but I decided to challenge myself and started writing. It didn't take me long to fill the page. I was surprised because here I was thinking I was miserable, yet I easily filled a page with things I was grateful for. And it felt good!

This little exercise got me going, and I found that I was constantly thinking of more things to be grateful for, and I just had to write them down. I wrote on scraps of paper in my purse, on the backs of receipts, and actually on anything that was handy when a thought came up. I finally bought a little journal and started to record things there. I was absolutely amazed that I kept coming up with new things, and the more new things I came up with, the better I felt, and I realized I was smiling. Knowing how good writing down my gratitude was making me feel made me want to share this feeling with others. I started paying attention when anyone did something I was grateful for, and I would express my gratitude right then. If someone held the door open for me, I thanked that person. When my hairdresser cut my hair, I told her how great it made me feel to have her do such a wonderful job. I even wrote notes to people to thank them for a variety of things they did that made my life easier or made me smile. The more grateful I became, the happier I became. I felt better. Most of my physical complaints subsided. I lost weight. And life in general felt good again. And I knew then that I would survive.

I examined my gratitude journey and decided to research if I was the only one who felt this way or if there was some science behind it. I was delighted to find that there is lots of research, and that everyone agrees that being grateful and actually acting on that gratitude actually creates measurable positive results. Here are some of the areas that improve:

1. You can expect more energy. Finding yourself sad most of the time is heavy. The tears and sorrow weigh you down. The positiveness of gratitude releases that weight from your shoulders, and you will find yourself more likely to want to do things. And I realized that the more I did, the better I felt.

2. You will be healthier. The more energy I had, and the more I used that energy to walk or swim or dance, the more my physical conditions improved. I discovered that the headaches I was having were from the position in which I was lying on the couch when I just couldn't convince myself to move. All I needed to do at that point to feel better was to get up off that couch. As hard as that was, I did, and I did feel much better.

3. You will be kinder. When we spend our time just thinking of ourselves, that's pretty miserable. But when we reach out to others, the kindness comes along. Today I called a friend who can't drive and asked her out to breakfast. She was so thrilled to get out of the house, and I was thrilled to spend time with her. That act of random kindness made the day for both of us, and all it took was a phone call.

4. Your work will be better. The more you recognize the gratitude you experience from working at your job or volunteering or creating things, the more productive you will be and the more pride you will take in what you do. Or you may realize that you are grateful to have had this work experience, and you will be grateful for a new work opportunity so you can move on to your next adventure.

5. Your creativity will flow. Whatever gifts and talents you have will open wide as you realize that these are gifts you can use to enhance your life experiences. I find that I can cook, paint, sew, sculpt, and write with ease when I am

smiling and being grateful for the inspiration that comes from being grateful for the process.

6. Your relationships will grow deeper. When you consistently and sincerely tell those around you what you appreciate about them and what they do, they are likely to start expressing gratitude also, not only to you, but to others around them. The ripple effect that occurs when you throw a rock into a calm lake is similar to the ripple effect that comes from an expression of gratitude. If you express your gratitude to someone for opening the door for you, that person is likely to thank the next person who opens the door for her or him. And more and more doors will be opened.

7. You will experience more joy. When I met Peggy, Shanesa, and Sarah at an event one evening, we discovered we were all experiencing loss. Among the four of us, we had experienced the deaths of many family members. And instead of expressing sorrow, we were expressing how grateful we were to have known the people before they died and the joy they brought into our lives. We realized that focusing on that joy instead of pain allowed our happy memories to come to the forefront.

8. You will notice gratitude all around you. I was out having lunch with Debbie today, and a young woman came up to my friend to tell her that she had been her dance teacher when she was very young, and that she loved her dance lessons which made such a positive impact on her life. Debbie had the biggest smile and was just thrilled by this unexpected gesture. Gratitude is a thing that, once you start practicing it and noticing when others express it, the world just seems full of positive thoughts and smiles, and you helped to make it all happen.

Taking Action with Your Gratitude

A few things are key to remember when you are expressing your gratitude. First, be spontaneous. You don't need to plan anything in advance. Just living with an attitude of gratitude will remind you to express your thanks and joy about situations as they arise. Thank your Uber driver when your ride ends. Thank your servers at a café when they bring your food. Thank your friend for calling you on the phone. You can even thank your flowers for their gorgeous blooms, your garden for its yummy vegetables, or the sky for its amazing blue color.

You can speak or write your gratefulness. You can express yourself to someone specific, or you can say something in general to a group. You can write a thank-you note, or you can write a list in your journal. Or, when you lie in bed at night, you can go over everything that happened that day that you are grateful for. This works much better than counting sheep to help you drift off to sleep. The method is not as important as the act. And practicing gratitude does not have to take a lot of time. As the Nike commercials say, "Just do it!"

Practice: Gratitude

At this point, you may be saying that you don't have anything to be grateful for. I understand that, but I encourage you to try this tool anyway. Before I started writing my own gratitude lists, I came to realize that that I was unconsciously making lots of lists of things I wasn't grateful for which I now call my Poor Me lists. I would dwell on how lonely I was, how terrible my alcoholic next-door neighbor was who abused his wife and encouraged his sons to fight, how I no longer had a job I loved because I gave it up to care for my dying husband, how my friends didn't call me, how I had no idea what to do next, and on and on and on. Those lists didn't serve me. So, I now write gratitude lists which do serve me. Now I am grateful I wake up in the morning. I am grateful for the beautiful place I live in. I am grateful to hear the birds singing every day. I am grateful that I can take a deep breath. I am grateful that I can write gratitude lists.

Try writing right now five things you are grateful for. No one will see them or judge you, so feel free to write anything you would like. Start each item with "I am grateful for," then complete the sentence. Do this every day. Try not to repeat things, but it is okay if you do. There are no rules here. Just gratitude.

Key Tips for Chapter 7

- There is always an abundance of things to be grateful for.
- Recognizing what you are grateful for results in physical and emotional benefits.
- Expressing gratitude brings much joy.

Chapter 8

Self-Love

"We're not meant to become perfect. We are meant to be whole."

—Jane Fonda

Taking care of yourself is essential. Take a bath, get a facial, or go for a walk. Find what really feels good to you and do that, often. Self-love, though, goes way beyond the superficial. Take a moment to really think about whether you actually love yourself. Most of us do love ourselves, but often that love isn't unconditional. So let's look at how we can bring more love into our lives.

First, how are you taking care of yourself? Early on, it's easy to get lost. We don't see ourselves in the mirror. We forget to smile. We forget that there is still joy to have in life. We may even forget to bathe and change clothes. If these things happen to you, know that they happen to lots of other people too. The key is to get to a point where you recognize that this is happening, and when you do, it's time to wake up. And when you do, know that it is time to focus on how to love yourself.

Start by taking a long, hot bath or shower. Wash and condition your hair. Put some nourishing lotion all over your body, and get dressed in something clean that you love. Then look at yourself in the mirror and smile. The smile may feel forced at first, but keep working it till it makes you giggle or laugh a bit. Then, staring at that beautiful face, say "I really love you lots!" You may need to go through this process several times before it feels natural. Then it starts to feel good, and you are on your way to living your best life!

How you feel about yourself affects everything in your life. If you don't fully love you, how can you expect anyone else to? How you relate to others depends on how you feel about you. For instance, family and friends will be happier and more eager to be around you when you demonstrate self-love by genuinely smiling and taking care of yourself. So, let's get started.

Self-love grows when we take action. Take steps to support and improve not only your physical being, but your psychological being and spiritual being as well. Start by deciding which area to focus on first. Then try one thing at a time to discover what works best for you, and find joy in the process. When we realize that we love ourselves and that we are lovable, we can discover and be more centered in our life's purpose. So how can you find your life's purpose? Up till now, you may have felt that purpose was serving the loved one who transitioned. When that is the case, you may feel lost. So now is the time to discover how to move forward.

Let's start with mindfulness. When you are mindful, you know or discover what you want for your life. For instance, if it seems that you have always had someone to love and that loved one has transitioned, what do you need to do to move forward? When we grieve someone we deeply love, that doesn't just end or go away, but we can be mindful of how we deal with what we feel and find a special place to store, remember, and celebrate that person. When you do that, you have more room to move forward. Focus on what you think, what you feel, and what you want. Be sure all of that supports you. Release anything that doesn't. For instance, if you think you are supposed to be sad, that doesn't serve you. If you think about what you need to do to feel strong and joyful, that does serve you. So really pay attention to what you are thinking and what you choose to do.

Now is the time to face inner challenges. Do you allow that monkey mind in your head to deprive you of the peace of meditation? Do you convince yourself that you are too fat, too thin, too lonely? Examine what you are thinking about, and discover what you need to do to make your self-talk positive in a way that supports you. Let go of old stories about how you aren't enough, and create new stories about how you are more than enough. Recognize where you are right now, and discover what you need to do to adjust that to where you want to be, knowing that you can move forward.

Are there things in your life now that exhaust or consume you? Losing yourself in your career or whatever you do can be counterproductive, because you end up so exhausted that you can't face anything else. That doesn't serve you, or the people you are working for, or the ones you are trying to impress. Try focusing on doing your very best while taking time to care for yourself by taking breaks, not working more than eight hours at a time, and by allowing the time and space you need to do quality work or to create something wonderful.

Are you doing what you want, what you love? One time in my life I had a career I loved, but I realized that the atmosphere around that career was toxic and that I had to leave. I was amazed at the way I felt after I quit. And once I released that job, a much better job fell into my lap. People at the new job told me they had been waiting for me to quit the old job so that they could offer me this perfect position. So, don't get in your own way. Life is full of possibilities, even if it feels differently.

Another way to be mindful is to treat others with love and respect. When my first boss, Bob, was orienting me to my new job, he told me to always treat my customers the way I would want to be treated. That advice served me well throughout my careers, but I eventually discovered that I could do better than that. Instead of following the golden rule, I switched to the platinum rule of treating my customers, patients, or students the best they could be treated because I realized I would love to be treated that way, too. Living with this attitude brings your life up a notch. I have had many people express their gratitude to me for how I treated them and what they learned from me.

Reaching out to others is an excellent way to practice self-care. Sometimes you just need someone to listen, or just be there so you aren't alone. Often, our friends and family don't reach out to us because they don't know what to do or say, but they probably would be thrilled if you contacted them and gave them something they could do. You may need someone to buy your groceries, or you may just want someone to sit quietly with you so that you don't feel so alone. If you need someone to help you or to be with you, reach out. And if the first person you ask is not available, ask another person. I had people say, "Just let me know if you need anything." Frequently we ignore that request, but chances are that if you do let the people who said this know what you need, they will be there for you.

Self-care also includes accepting who you are right now. We all have memories of our lives before now that included the roles we may have had then but don't now. When my mother died, a friend pointed out to me that I became an orphan. That statement made me feel terrible. I had always been a daughter, but that role was no longer mine. However, as I contemplated my situation, I saw that my mom and dad will always be my parents whether they are here in a physical body or not, so I will always be their daughter. Many of the tasks I had, however, were no longer necessary, so I just needed to realign my life to where I am now. The time I had spent caring for them, taking them to the doctor, or paying bills was now freed up for me to care for myself and participate more fully in the roles I actively play now.

You will discover new relationships as you move forward in your life. When you meet people, consider whether you want to take the time to be a good friend. If a person you meet has the traits you admire and you want to be around, then pursue that relationship with open arms and an open heart. When you find yourself in the company of people who do not line up with your values and goals, you can be polite, but you don't need to form a relationship. I once was in a position where those around me had values that I could not support. By leaving that position, I not only felt better about myself since I wasn't constantly exposed to the negativity, but I actually felt joy and acceptance when I met new people who accepted me as I am. A good way to find these new relationships is to consciously be the person you want to be—then you will attract people like you. And if you still have relationships with people who work against you or take pleasure in your pain, release those relationships. They don't serve you.

Now is the time to decide what you really want to do and what you really want to be. Have you always wanted to advance your education? Have you always wanted to take dance lessons? Have you always wanted to change your career or retire? Do you want to expand your spiritual practice? Do you want to learn to paint, or sculpt, or surf, or play tennis? Now is the time. Take time to explore the concept of what you really want. When you focus on your dreams and desires consistently and actually take action to move forward, the world will open up for you. Be realistic, and take charge of your life.

A huge part of self-love is taking care of your body with how you eat and how you exercise. Keep track for a few days of every single thing you eat. Then notice if you are eating a balanced diet, if you are eating processed foods, if you are eating too much or not eating enough. Now is a good time to look at nutrition. I did, and I became a vegetarian because, when I really looked at what I was eating, I just couldn't eat animals anymore. And I have gone further to eat vegan most of the time. I still do just love cheese, but I am working on it. And after you look at the energy you consume, examine the energy you expend. Do you exercise? If you do, how can you improve your routine to better serve your body? If you don't, what do you need to do to get started? The easiest way is to start walking and gradually increase your distance. I joined a water aerobics class that not only helped my whole body get stronger, I also met some wonderful people. The key to eating well and staying fit is to do it! You can! I have faith in you!

Make everything you do a part of your self-love. If you find yourself doing something that doesn't serve you, stop. If you find yourself endlessly playing solitaire, switch that out for reading a book or taking a walk. If you feel lonely, call a friend or find a place to volunteer. Think of yourself as your most precious loved one and treat yourself as if you are. Life is good. Love it!

Practice: Self-Care

Plan a Self-Care Day. Have fun with this. Start by making a list of everything you can think of that would feel wonderful for you to do just for you. Here are some ideas:

- Get a massage
- Get a facial

- Buy a new outfit
- Take a bubble bath
- Spend the day with a special friend
- Take a class
- Write a story
- Take yourself to lunch at a restaurant you have been wanting to try
- Go for a hike
- Read a good book
- Watch a movie you've been wanting to see

I could go on and on, but I want you to make a list of your own. Feel free to get wild and crazy with your list. When you are finished, use your list to inspire the design of your special day. Then set a date, and do whatever you design. You will love how it all turns out, and I encourage you to do this for yourself at least once a month. Enjoy!

Key Points for Chapter 8

- Unconditional love for yourself is essential.
- Discover who you really are.
- Reaching out to others is healthy.

Chapter 9

Judgment

"Never judge others. You both know good and well how unexpected
events can change who a person is. Always keep that in mind. You
never know what someone else is experiencing within their own life."

—Colleen Hoover, *Slammed*

Jacques and I were well-known in our community for many
years and were a well-known couple. After he died, I still felt
like I was known as Jacques's wife. That was my perception,
and it led me to think that, if I was seen with someone else,
people would talk. And I really didn't want anyone saying that
I was rushing things. Really, I didn't want to be judged. I knew
a lovely man, Adrian, who told me that he understood that it
might be hard for me to go to places or events by myself, so
he asked me to call him when I wanted company. That helped
me, and I appreciated his kindness and generosity. However,
one night he accompanied me to an event, and I actually heard
people saying things like that it was too soon for me to be
dating someone and that I was probably relieved when Jacques
died because now I could get on with my life. I was stunned.
How could anyone say such things? And I did let it affect me. I
became overly concerned about what others thought and said.

When I met Ron, I believed I was ready for a new relationship, yet at the same time, I caught myself not ready to be seen with him in public for fear of what people would think. I didn't tell Ron I felt this way, but it did slow down the development of our relationship. I am grateful that Ron was patient with me and stuck with me long enough for me to be thrilled to be seen with him in public and not worry about what anyone said. I realized at this time that, not only did I feel the perceived judgment of others, I was actually judging myself. And I realized I had to give up judgment, which was not an easy task.

This story by the Brazilian novelist Paulo Coelho is a perfect example of judging others:

> A young couple moved into a new neighbourhood. The next morning while they were eating breakfast, the young woman saw her neighbour hanging the washing outside.
>
> "That laundry is not very clean; she doesn't know how to wash correctly. Perhaps she needs better laundry soap."
>
> Her husband looked on, remaining silent. Every time her neighbour hung her washing out to dry, the young woman made the same comments.
>
> A month later, the woman was surprised to see a nice clean wash on the line and said to her husband, "Look, she's finally learned how to wash correctly. I wonder who taught her this."
>
> The husband replied, "I got up early this morning and cleaned our windows."

Have you ever caught yourself doing something similar? How many times have you realized that you were judging someone else? I have directed many plays, and as a director, my job was to evaluate the performances of the actors during rehearsals and let them know what they could do to improve the production. I also taught writing for years at the university level, and my job was to evaluate student writing and tell them what they can do to improve. I realized that I was translating this type of evaluation frequently to other areas of my life. I was telling people what they should do and thinking about what people should be doing. Then one day I told Christine, a friend, what she should do. She looked at me very sternly and said, "Don't you should on me!" That interaction shocked me and led me to self-evaluation.

I realized that what I thought was my effort to help people was actually just a way of judging them. I knew I didn't like to be judged, so I started making a serious effort not to judge others. As I released judgment of others, I saw how much I was judging myself, and I had to learn to release that, too.

So, you are probably wondering what this has to do with how you are feeling right now. Lots. First, we tend to judge ourselves harshly in events surrounding death. Karen, a widow of two years, told me of the anguish she felt around leaving her husband at the hospital to take care of things at home and having him die alone while she was away. She also judged herself for not being able to get him to talk more about his impending passing. And she felt guilty for not being more patient with him and about not being more assertive on his behalf. Another example of self-judgment was when Tanisha felt that she was in some way responsible for her husband's suicide because she had not realized he was depressed. Many of us share similar feelings in conjunction with our experience of loss.

When you carefully examine your actions and thoughts, you may discover that you have been judging others subconsciously, not realizing that in the moment. Some things that incorporate judgment are:

1. You fail to listen to what someone is telling you, dismissing what they are saying.

2. You participate in gossip which may not be the truth.

3. You don't allow others to criticize you.

4. You do not forgive another's thoughts or actions, and if you do forgive, you don't forget what they have said or done.

5. You judge someone by a job or education rather than who that person really is.

When you recognize things like this are forms of judgment, you may realize that you are judging others much more than you thought you were. Frequently we make a judgment before we have complete information, and we most frequently judge others in areas where we feel the weakest. So, if you are realizing that this is an area you would like to work on, here are some ways you can take action:

1. Forgive yourself for anything you have been judging yourself for.

2. Really listen when others are speaking to you. When you find that you are judging what they are saying, ask yourself what other information you need so that you won't feel the need to be judgmental.

3. Be mindful of what you say and do.

4. Don't take things personally.

5. Examine carefully what you are doing and saying.

6. See things as they really are.

I went through much of my life assuming that, if I knew things, everyone else did too, or if I could do things, everyone else could too. This did not serve me. I was not assessing how things actually were. I first realized I was doing this when I assumed that, if I followed a recipe and it turned out well, then anyone else could do the same thing. This just isn't true. I would share a recipe and when someone else made it, it was not like what I made. So, if you see that someone else who has suffered a loss isn't dealing with that loss the way you do, that does not make either one of you right or wrong. You are different, and that's okay. Judgment is not needed here.

If you realize that you are having unkind thoughts about someone, examine those thoughts. More often than not, you are likely to discover that what you are criticizing in someone else is actually a problem that you have. So be honest with yourself, and be tender with yourself. The more you can identify your issues, the easier it will be for you to deal with them and step back to take a wider view.

These examples indicate the danger of judging others:

1. Inadequate information. For instance, you may see someone who appears drunk to you when that person may not have been drinking at all, but rather is in a life-threatening medical crisis.

2. People are different. If you don't understand how people can waste so much time watching sports because you don't enjoy sports, that doesn't mean that the person who does enjoy sports is bad or wrong.

3. The golden rule. When you know you could say something to someone that you would be appalled to have someone say to you, realize that before you say it, and don't. And if it does get past your lips, apologize.

4. What you think you see may not be the truth. When
    I had my theatre, the first person to purchase season
    tickets from me was a man who appeared to be homeless,
    with raggedy clothes and hats and messy hair. When he
    came to a production, someone would always complain
    to me that a homeless man had snuck in. So I would
    explain that this man was one of my biggest supporters,
    always buying season tickets and coming to see
    every production.

5. Learn tolerance. Just because someone does not have
    the same interests as you or the same priorities you have
    does not mean that they are bad or wrong.

As you release both giving and receiving judgment from
your life, you will experience a sense of peace and freedom that
will transform your life experience. People tend to judge others
by how they think others are supposed to act. If you feel judged,
it is not your problem. People are going to think whatever they
want to think. Just do what is right for you always.

Practice: Releasing Judgment

To release judgment, you first will discover areas where you are
judging. Make a list of everything in your life right now where
you are holding judgment against someone or something. Here
are some ideas for inspiration:

- You are bothered that a friend has not been there to
  support you in your loss

- You feel your loved one could have lived longer if he
  had exercised and eaten better

- You feel your friend got married much too soon after
  her husband died

- You feel your neighbor is ruining the neighborhood because she doesn't mow her lawn

- You feel your child could do better in school if only she tried harder

Now look at each of these hypothetical statements and come up with a genuine possible cause for each situation that is either something you couldn't have known, or if you did know the reason, you would understand.

Now make your list and, for each item on the list, whether you know all the facts or not, release your feelings of judgment because those feelings are not serving you. In the process, you might even discover a way you could make a difference for the person you were judging.

Key Points for Chapter 9

- Recognize when you judge others and stop judging.
- Recognize when others judge you.
- Release judgment from your life.

Chapter 10

Being Social

"The present moment is all you ever have."

—Eckhardt Tolle

While grieving, initially, it's natural to want to be alone. For me, the thought of going out of my house for just about anything was overwhelming. My comfy bed called me to cuddle up with pillows, or my television talked to me through my favorite characters on the shows I was watching. The actual effort it took to go out of my home was almost overwhelming. Having to get dressed and comb my hair to look presentable in public just didn't seem worth it. Yet I recognized that this behavior wasn't serving me. I knew I couldn't escape from the world, and in truth, I didn't really want to. But I wasn't used to going anyplace alone. I didn't know what to do or how to act.

Then one day, through self-reflection, I realized that I was alone because I wasn't doing anything to improve my situation. I started writing in my journal, exploring what I could do, what I would like to do, and what I would really love to do. Things I could do were to meditate daily, plan my meals with new recipes and grocery shop, or go for a walk on the beach.

Things I would like to do were to meditate with friends, share my interests, and walk with someone on the beach. Exploring these ideas and how I would love to experience them, I invited friends to meditate with me every morning, invited friends to my home where I would teach them vegan cooking, and invited a friend to walk with me on the beach. Explore what works for you.

I recalled how Jacques used to tell me of his experiences with meetings of the group he facilitated for the Bereaved Persons Association. He recalled one woman who attended every time, and every time, she sobbed while she told the story of her daughter who had died. Other people shared horrific experiences of dealing with loss through murder, accidents, and suicide. He said that these people kept coming, and they gradually cried less and stepped into the role of comforting others. While some people attended only once, many stayed the course and were grateful for the comfort of being with others who shared loss. But, recalling the stories that Jacques told me, I just couldn't face meeting with strangers and plunging into the depths of their losses of their loved ones.

Then someone told me about a local Death Café. Although I had not heard of this concept before, the first Death Café was in 2004 in Switzerland and was created to break the secrecy around death, to get people talking. People who were interested in talking about death or learning more about death would get together and talk over tea and cake. Those who attended did not have to be grieving, just curious, so I decided to go to a meeting. Led by Bodhi Be, the group was objective, and we even found moments to laugh and just breathe over guacamole and beer. I met two women there who I had things in common with who made me feel so comfortable. And I loved the range of ages of the attendees. And even though their stories of deaths included accidents, suicide, cancer, and more, we celebrated the lives of our loved ones so positively that I left that evening smiling and exhaling.

Check out your community to see what is available, and expand your search beyond things you are familiar with to things you have always wanted to do. Then pick one thing and try it. And if that ends up not suiting you, try something else. I always thought that paddle boarding looked so peaceful and easy, but when I tried it, I realized that it requires great balance, and after landing in the coral when I fell off the board, I decided there were other things I could try! Don't stop. Keep trying new things. Take an art class, or travel.

I love ceramics. And I love to travel, so I discovered a tour of Tuscany where we would attend the international ceramics festival and competition, visit museums and churches to observe ceramics through history, and spend time taking hands-on classes in studios. So I signed up and looked forward to my journey for six months. On the trip, the best part was all the women I met, several of whom are widows. We had the opportunity to get to know each other not only through our common loss, but also through our common love of ceramics. I am grateful that I went on this journey to do something really different and met new lifetime friends.

So, what would you like to do? Here are a few ideas:

- Set up a picnic or potluck where old and new friends can come together without the expectation of people being in couples.

- Sign up for a class to learn something you have always wanted to, like ceramics, computers, cooking, literature, or investing.

- Join an organization, like a political party, a hiking club, a philanthropical group, or a book club.

- Build and strengthen relationships you already have by scheduling a regular time to get together with a friend, inviting a friend for a walk or for tea, or inviting a friend to try a new restaurant with you or go to a movie.

- Set up a schedule to regularly email someone who would love to hear from you, like a friend who has recently moved, someone who recently went away to college, a good friend you haven't heard from in years, or someone who is going through a tough time.

- Practice self-care, like going to the gym, taking a water aerobics or aerial class, or regular walks with a friend.

Take some time now to look at how you are spending your time. For a few days, write down what you do every hour. Discover any patterns you may have—you may work from eight to five, come home and fix something to eat, then collapse in front of the television. Or you may binge-read books or play video games. Or you may be taking lots of naps. You may eat mindlessly out of boredom. You may find that you constantly keep yourself busy out of fear of not having something to do. Does any of this sound like you? The way you fill your time may be entirely different from any of these, so just look at what you do. What would you like to stop doing? What would you like to start doing? Now make a plan.

I talked to many people who were grieving, and I discovered that there was no particular timetable as to when to be social again. Nina said that she and her husband had enjoyed going out together and it took her a while to start going out alone. After two years, she started going to concerts and the theater alone, and I met her on the ceramics tour of Tuscany that I went on a year after Ron died. Being in a group of people who enjoy something that you do is a great way to start trying something new or different.

When I asked Marla how she started getting back into the swing of things, she said:

> First, I started taking classes—in tai chi, yoga, Zumba, weights, Spanish, stone carving, cake decorating—and attended concerts, plays. I still take Spanish and weights; knee problems keep me from tai chi and yoga. (No talent for carving and don't need the temptation of cakes.)
>
> Next, I accepted an invitation to join the Advisory Board of Concord Carlisle Adult and Community Education and participate in several projects.
>
> More recently, I joined Overeaters Anonymous, where I've made several friends. My weight is okay, but I've found valuable fellowship in meeting with others who use food for uses other than nutrition, especially in making new friends. I plan to join a few book clubs and take more classes.

Marla did a lot. She tried some things that worked and some that didn't, and she was not concerned about what anyone else thought about what she was doing. That's important, because right now, you are taking care of you. I know that, for years, there were things that I passed up because of my husbands' health, and now I can do those things. For instance, I have walked more in the past two weeks than I have in years because their health prevented them from walking, so I sat with them. Think about something you haven't been doing that you always wanted to, and get started on it, now.

Maryann's husband died three years ago. At first, she had difficulty with commitment. After Michael, her husband, died, her friend Kevin Wallace would go to the farmers' market for her. She'd tell him, "Only get cherry tomatoes, a full-size tomato is too large a commitment for me; baby steps." But gradually, she was ready for more. "I got involved in Focus on the Masters (a nonprofit arts support foundation) Gala Fundraisers. Art workshops. Intellectual workshops. Workshops are safe because you can interact as little or as much as you want. You can stay quiet if you're not feeling brave, or you can interact with other participants and make new friends and contacts if you are. Workshops are also great because you can choose a one-day workshop or several hours workshop or weeklong workshop, depending on how you're feeling, so the commitment is small. Whereas, if you take a course at a university or something the commitment is large, too big. Being social is a tough one."

Start with what you feel you can handle, then move on from there. I am loving making new friends and getting involved in things I care about. Invite someone or a couple of people for tea, or wine, or dinner, and just visit. This can feel so good. Then just go where you want to go, and do what you want to do.

Practice: Plan an Event

To be social, you need to do something social, and one way to do this is to plan your own event. Here are some ideas you could try:

- Plan to go to brunch with three friends.

- Host a luncheon at your house where everyone brings their favorite salad and you provide drinks and dessert, and be sure to plan a little activity you can all do together and have a fun little gift for everyone who attends.

- Plan a yard party for your neighborhood where you can have a barbecue and children and pets are welcome.

- Get together with a couple of friends to go on a beautiful walk.

- Ask a few friends to go to a concert or play with you.

- Take a class with a friend or two in watercolors, photography, guitar, dance, paddling, or anything that strikes your fancy.

The key here is to get out with other people and have fun. I recently went to a Michael Franti concert with three friends, and we are still talking about how much fun we had! Just plan something and do it, and if you invite someone who can't come, just ask someone else, and make new friends too!

Key Points for Chapter 10

- Go where you want to go.
- Do what you want to do.
- Find ways to connect with others.

Chapter 11

Loneliness

"We're all in this alone."

—Lily Tomlin

Most of my life has been spent living either with my family, before I got married, or living with a husband. I had no idea what living by myself would be like, and I hadn't really thought of it. But then the time came when I was alone, and I truly didn't know how to live by myself. Since I didn't have someone to share meals with, I frequently forgot to eat and lost lots of weight. I did not like to go out by myself and did not know where to go by myself anyway. I spent lots of time generally in despair. I finally decided that this was no way to live and started changing.

Realizing that you are not alone, even though you may feel lonely, can make all the difference. Everybody experiences loss throughout their lives. Lots of people probably love you and are here for you but may not know what to say or have any idea of when you need them. So, be mindful of when you start to feel lonely. Sometimes you will want to spend some time with someone and sometimes you will want to spend some time in solitude, to meditate, to be with yourself and discover who you are now in your present circumstances, to spend time loving yourself. Solitude can be a wonderful experience.

Loneliness is different from solitude. Loneliness can find you wallowing in the sorrow of missing your loved one. No one else will experience exactly what you are feeling, as no one else had the same relationship with your loved one who died, whether it was your husband, your child, your parent, your partner, your unborn child, or your friend. Feeling alone is not unusual. When my first pregnancy ended at twenty weeks, I didn't know anyone else who had lost a baby or had a miscarriage. I thought something like this was extremely unusual and that I had no one to relate to. Even my husband was absent, finding reasons to be away from home. Many months later, he finally admitted to me that he was having very similar feelings and hadn't expressed them to me because he felt that he had somehow failed me, as I felt I had failed him. I realized then that, had we only been able to talk to each other, we could have comforted each other, rather than being so lonely. And I eventually discovered that many people I knew had dealt with miscarriages, but at that time people just didn't talk about it.

Can you think of someone who can be there for you now? Try calling, writing, or texting someone and letting them know you could really use a friend. While actually being with someone can be wonderful, just being in touch with someone can help too. We moved to Maui two years before Ron died, and I have met some wonderful people here, but I found myself longing for my friends who lived far away. I discovered that, if I texted or called or wrote, they would respond, and they were grateful to do so. Many times, when people don't know what to say, or it feels like they are giving you your space, they actually are just waiting to hear from you and are happy to be in touch.

And I know that who you are really lonely for is that person you can no longer call, or talk to, or be with. What you feel is that empty space that had been filled by the one you loved. You shared so much that no one else knows, and now you feel like a piece of you is missing. You can't pick up the phone to call your mom who died from cancer to tell her something special. You can't share with your husband who died in an accident something that made you smile today. Or you can't have a birthday party for your child who drowned. This is the kind of loneliness that comes from loss, and it isn't something you can solve. You can, however, over a period of time, learn to deal with this loneliness by opening yourself to love. This love isn't necessarily romantic but can come from becoming comfortable with loving yourself. Find a way to express your love. Here are some ideas people have used to actively deal with their loneliness:

1. Angela fell in love with an adorable Labrador puppy. She discovered that training the puppy, taking the puppy for walks, and cuddling with the puppy brought her great peace and joy.

2. Jodie volunteered at the nursery at her local hospital by rocking babies whose parents couldn't always be with them.

3. Hal, a contractor, spent time working with an organization building homes for the homeless.

4. Anisha worked with Big Brothers/Big Sisters in a program to befriend foster children.

5. Cordell volunteered at a local botanical garden helping to keep it weed-free and planting new flowers.

6. Shelby took time to actively learn to love herself by practicing smiling and walking every day.

7. Francesca rented out two rooms in her house to friends who discovered that they loved communal living, sharing meals and household chores.

Another thing you can do is learn to have fun by yourself. I loved doing aqua Zumba. Something about dancing in the water where no one could see what I was doing was freeing. And find things that will make you laugh. When you start to feel lonely, trying searching YouTube for funny things animals do. Sometimes they are just too hysterical not to laugh at.

In the movie *Like Father*, the father character is dealing with the death of his best friend and business partner. One line he says is, "Fear of loneliness is a powerful thing." Sometimes we become so wrapped up in the fear of what may happen that we neglect to deal with where we actually are right now. Are you actually lonely, or are you fearing that loneliness will come? It could be that, at this moment, you do have a friend or family member you could spend some time with. When you start to feel lonely, consider who that person would be. Ask them out for coffee or to go to a movie with you. Or invite them over so that you can cook dinner. Make the effort to actually connect with someone. That connection may actually change your lives. At the very least, you will be actively taking steps to enhance your life.

In the famous graduation speech Steve Jobs made for Stanford, he said, "You can't connect the dots looking forward; you can only connect them looking backward. So you have to trust that the dots will somehow connect in your future. You have to trust in something—your gut, destiny, life, karma, whatever. This approach has never let me down, and it has made all the difference in my life."

What are your dots? Spend some time examining how the life experiences of your past have led to your present experiences. What decisions have you made before that brought you joy? How did you establish relationships with the people who became your friends, your very best friends, or your spouse? What can you do now to foster relationships you already have or relationships that you can discover that will help you deal with the void you are feeling now?

Missing your loved one is inevitable, yet being lonely is not. I am not saying that it is easy, but you can decide for yourself what you can actively do to keep or bring human connection into your life. Chose to do something now!

Practice: Connect the Dots

Steve Jobs's philosophy of connecting your dots can show how the events in your life worked together to get you to where you are today, and they can also give you an idea of where to go from here. Try examining something you have done and where it led you. An example for me was becoming a nurse. I wanted a career that I could train for quickly because my husband at the time had become a police officer, and we had two babies. After attending the funeral of one of his coworkers and knowing another who was shot, I wanted some security for my family in case something happened to him.

At the time, there were so many registered nurses that it would take me three years to start the programs I had been accepted in, so I went to the licensed vocational nursing program (in most states, this is known as practical nursing) with the intention of entering the RN program as soon as I finished. Because my husband was suffering from a major health problem, I wasn't able to do that. At the time, I was frustrated, but this led me indirectly to a different, wonderful job, a different education path leading to a master's degree and my writing career, and I had the much-needed medical training that helped me care for my mother, my aunt,

Jacques, my mother-in-law, and Ron, as well as many friends and neighbors.

When I did this exercise that led me to see how all the dots connected from just this one instance of deciding to become a nurse to lead me on an unpredictable path to a great life, I also noticed that it indirectly led me to my current passion of helping others reclaim their joy.

Choose one area in your life and discover how it is related to other areas by connecting the dots.

Key Points for Chapter 11

- Although we may be alone, we don't have to be lonely.

- Discover who you want to spend time with.

- Realize that only you can eliminate your loneliness.

Chapter 12

Joy

"Don't cry because it's over, smile because it happened."
—Dr. Seuss

Most agree that joy is an integral part of our humanness, as essential to life as breath. But dealing with loss is as well. Joy and loss lie at the opposite ends of the spectrum of our life experiences. With birth there is joy, and with death there is loss. Fully experiencing the power of joy allows you to fully recognize the depths of your loss, while fully participating in your feelings of loss allows you to fully experience the heights of joy. Joy and grief are yin and yang; they fit perfectly together. When you don't experience one fully, chances are you won't experience the other fully, either.

When Isolde and her husband Gerald found that they were expecting a daughter after having two sons, they were thrilled, and immediately decorated their nursery in pink. When they learned that their baby had died in utero, they were devastated. When they returned from the hospital, their two little boys ran up to them with hugs and sloppy kisses, so happy to see their parents. Isolde and Gerald found themselves smiling and

holding these sweet boys in big hugs. Going from the height
of joy to the pit of grief, they were able to rebound to the joy
of the precious family they had. Being happy in this family did
not negate the joy or the pain that they had experienced earlier.
It did allow them to feel the depths of the highs and the lows
while settling in a place where they could move forward.

Highs and lows are inevitable. Growing up in my family,
with lots of cousins and aunts and uncles, funerals were always
a big thing. We would have the service at the mortuary or
church, go to the cemetery, then return to a family member's
house to have a feast. In one day, we all joined in tears in the
morning, then laughter in the afternoon. As cousins played
together, elders shared stories of the dearly departed. Everyone
enjoyed the abundance of family favorite foods. We all still were
grieving and greatly missed the person who had transitioned,
but we rode the waves of joy and loss together, strengthening
each other in the process.

Recognizing our joy is important in our lives. Ron and I
spent endless hours sitting outside, holding hands, enjoying
the beauty of where we lived, the songs of the birds, the gentle
trade winds. In the evenings I would rub his feet, practicing
the reflexology I had learned to ease his pain. And we loved
snuggling in each other's arms as we drifted off to sleep.
Those days were filled with joy as we focused on those present
moments. After his transition, the loneliness of his absence
from our lanai and our bed was where I felt the most profound
sadness. Going through the highs and lows of these experiences
allowed me to fully feel what was happening. And it took time
to rise up from the depths of this loss, but now I feel myself
easily smiling, making new friends, doings things I haven't
done before, and coming back to life myself.

Think about times when you have experienced joy and grief
at the same time. My niece's grandfather died at the same time

she was getting married. We didn't discover his passing until we arrived home after the wedding. We were thrilled for my niece at the same time we grieved for my brother-in-law's loss of his father. While the feeling of one tempered the other, we all experienced a sense of joy and pain at the same time.

When Ron went on hospice and his friends and family gathered, we spent a week celebrating with Ron, sharing the joy of the life experiences we all had together. We also knew that we were saying goodbye at the same time. I still cry when I think of that week, even though it was a perfect experience.

Our ability to step back and see what is actually happening in our lives gives us the opportunity to relish the joyful experiences but also to grieve when the time comes. You may say, "But what do I have to be happy about?" The answer is, plenty! Be open and look for the experiences, for the moments that make you smile, that make your heart sing.

Here are a few ways I find joy in my life. As you read them, think of ways you can discover joy for yourself.

1. Take good care of yourself. Take a bubble bath, hug a friend, sit outside and have a glass of wine.

2. Exercise in whatever way works best for you. Go for a walk. Go for a swim. Go to the beach.

3. Celebrate, either by yourself or with friends. Who is having a birthday, had a baby, or got a promotion? Balloons and cake are called for!

4. Contribute when the need arises. With all the storms, fires, volcanoes, and the pandemic, someone always needs help. Volunteering time and giving money both can make a tremendous difference, even in small quantities.

5. Volunteer either regularly or for a special event. Help with giving rides to people so they can vote.

Cook a casserole for a shut-in friend. Spend time at a community garden.

6. Smile. You never know when you can change someone's day with a friendly word and a smile.

7. Practice unconditional love. No judgment, just joy!

8. Commit to actively practice pursuing joy.

You will find that opportunities arise all around you. When my daughter Abby was very young, her friend Sheila was terminally ill with cancer. Her bones were so brittle that when her brother tripped over her when she was lying on the floor, the resulting broken bones put her in a full body cast. My daughter would go to her house after school and sit with her, read her stories, and play with dolls. This experience brought joy to the little girl, her family, and my daughter. My daughter handled her friend's death really well. I know that feeling she had made a difference in the final days of her friend set her on a course of compassion for the rest of her life. Allowing children to actively participate in the activities of living and dying is so much more helpful than shielding them from the realities of life.

I once got a call from my friend Helen, telling me that one of her friends was taking care of her terminally ill mother in her home and really needed a break. She knew I was a nurse and thought maybe I could help. Even though I didn't know the family, I went to their house when they asked for me. I gave the mother a morphine shot (which was the way relief was provided at home at the time). As I was bathing her, I recognized when she took her last breath. The mother was undressed, with the family in the next room. I respectfully completed her bath, dressed her in her fresh white nightgown, changed her bed, and positioned her in a peaceful pose. Then I went to tell the family what had happened. They were so grateful to see her clean and fresh and at peace. Midwifing her through this process brought me great joy.

Jacques's granddaughter Katie and her husband Matt are professional jazz musicians. They enjoyed taking a break from their international touring by visiting me in Maui, where they could just relax. We asked them to do a concert a few months after Ron's transition. Getting to experience their fabulous talent in their performance brought me out of the funk I had been in and helped me breathe in joy and peace again. They brought with them for their performance Justin Kauflin, a jazz pianist who had become blind when he was eleven years old. I had the opportunity to sit on my lanai alone with him. We sat for a while in silence, at least the silence of not speaking, when he said to me that this was the most beautiful place he had ever experienced. He went on to describe the varied songs of the birds, the soft rings of all the different wind chimes, the rustle of the leaves from the trade winds, and the tinkle of the water in the fountain. I was struck by the joy of the beauty he was experiencing—not sensing any sorrow for what he could not see but reveling in the unseen beauty. I realized then that there was so much in life for me to enjoy, and I had to place my attention there.

Julie told me what helped her the most was when a friend offered, or more demanded, that she hand over her children so that Julie could nap, cry, take care of paperwork, or do whatever was needed. She also appreciated it when her friend stayed with her after her loved one's body was taken away. Staying to share memories. Staying to cry together, to laugh together. And she loved it when people showed up without an invitation just to give her a hug.

Jeanette H. told me that, after her loss, "I had no support and two children in the house to raise alone. I'm not sure how I survived. My art was always my refuge." Find your refuge by

diving into whatever it is that brings you joy. A refuge I have
is when my friends gather every morning for meditation. Part
of what we do is to share one joy we had the day before. The
joy can be anything from making cookies to getting a letter
or call from a friend. Maybe a stranger smiled at you and that
triggered you to smile back. Joys can be really simple or really
big! Recognize at least one joy a day. I even keep a list so that
I can refer back to it if I start to get a little down. What is your
joy today?

Staying open to joy, to beauty, to love, brightens all of your
life experiences. Being mindful of these opportunities will
greatly enhance your life.

Practice: Joy

My favorite thing to do every day socially is to get together first
thing in the morning to read, meditate, and meet with friends,
and to tell each other something that brought us joy the day
before. We often smile and laugh as we are talking about our
joy. It's a great way to start the day. I find myself thinking
about my joy all day so that I can remember something special
to share the next day. And I always write at least one joy for the
day, in my journal. Often, several. Think about what happened
yesterday. What made you smile? I've written about spending
time with friends, getting a special phone call, seeing a
beautiful rainbow, going to Farmer's Market, going to the gym,
walking on the beach, cooking my favorite dish, taking a bath,
meditating and so much more. If you are struggling as you
try to find joy, do something today that brings you joy so that
you can write about it tomorrow. Bring more joy into your life.
Paying attention to joy actually brings you more joy!

Key Tips for Chapter 12

- Joy is as essential as breath.
- Be mindful of the joy you experience.
- Discover moments of joy every day.

Chapter 13

The Stages of Grief

"That which is to give light must endure burning."
—Victor Frankl

You probably have heard of the five stages of grief. Elisabeth
Kubler-Ross developed the five stages when she was
researching death and dying, but, over the years, this concept
has been attached to grief. The stages also apply to different
kinds of loss and stress. Up to this time, grief was rarely spoken
of, so in applying the stages to grief, people were happy that
they had something to hold onto, so they would know how
long this grief thing would last. It doesn't work that way. Now
you can find lists of anywhere from three and nine stages of
grief, and most researchers and counselors agree that the grief
process is not linear and follows no specific pattern. Sometimes
we start with anticipatory grief, as in Carla's case when her
father was put on hospice after surgery at age ninety-three. She
and her mother started grieving then, yet her father lived five
more years. There is no specific time to start or end the grieving
process. We all probably go through some form of five stages:

1. Denial and isolation

2. Anger

3. Bargaining

4. Depression

5. Acceptance

We may not ever hit all of those steps. Other researchers have added and subtracted stages along the way. And all these stages don't necessarily come in that or any order, and they may repeat and may be simultaneous. You don't need to search these experiences out. There is no graduation after fulfilling the requirements. Just take the steps you need to, knowing that along the way, the path will constantly change. And that's okay.

Dealing with loss is a rich, sweet experience when we allow it to be. While emotions like sorrow are frequently equated with grieving, grief is so much more than that. As we go through the process of grieving, we have the opportunity to recount all the wonderful things we love about our life experience with our loved one. You can remember events like weddings, anniversaries, births, and celebrations. You can remember characteristics of your loved one, like compassion, service, integrity, and faith. You can remember everyday joys like dancing in the kitchen, snuggling at bedtime, holding hands, and never letting a day go by without saying "I love you." Keeping in mind the joy you can discover, let's explore the traditional stages to see how recognizing them can serve you.

Denial: When someone we love dies, the fact that they are actually not here (in the form of their body) anymore takes a while to register in our thinking. Often it seems that they are just asleep, or in the other room, or not home yet from work or school. Something will happen that you want to share, and when you go to tell them, you can't. Our brains don't easily shift from the presence of our loved ones to their absence. And sometimes in this stage we may deal with it by unconsciously going numb or being confused. This is denial. Some experts combine shock and denial into one stage. Shock is your natural defense mechanism to protect you. Shock can last for weeks or months and will gradually subside.

Denial can come both before and after death. Jacques was a bioethicist whose specialty was death and dying, and though his life's work involved studying all things about death and dying, when the time came for him, he really didn't realize that he was going to die until about an hour before his death. He dealt with his health struggles as something he had to go through to get better. His denial made communicating difficult because we never could talk about the possibility of his not always being alive. When he died, I didn't feel so much denial as relief that his struggle and suffering was over.

Julie shared this story of her denial: "I was one of two family members who stayed at Grandma's bedside during her many hospital stays. Not that other family members didn't care, but for various reasons and life circumstances, they were visitors and not caregivers. We had a small memorial service for her a couple of months after she passed away. Family and a few friends gathered to eat together and share memories. I sat and listened to everyone share such colorful, rich, and precious stories. And I sat. And I sat some more. I could not get myself up to share any of my precious memories. I could not tie the bow on that package. Perhaps that's what my denial looked like."

Anger: Anger can be displayed in many ways. Maybe your loved one promised to buy a cord of firewood and get it stacked, ready for a cozy fire in the cold weather, but that didn't get done, and when the cold night comes, when all you want to do it sit by the fire, there's no wood, no one to build the fire—a task he always enjoyed—and you are suddenly furious, first that you are cold, and then that he is not there. Or you may become angry when your friend says the wrong thing or doesn't invite you to a dinner where there will only be couples. There are lots of things that come up that cause anger to flare. Don't be surprised.

I was angry before Jacques died when we went to a car lot to pick up a new car we had purchased. The temperature outside was over 100 degrees that day, so all the employees were inside the building. As we walked toward the showroom, Jacques became weak and passed out. I was able to get behind him and ease him to the ground while screaming for help. I kept screaming, but no help came. I finally had to lay him on the hot pavement while I ran inside to tell them to call 911 and get outside to help me. In that short time, the hot asphalt had given him second-degree burns all over his back. I was furious at the dealership because there was no one to help us when we needed it and mad at myself for our decision to purchase a car at this point, even though we hadn't known that his health was going to decline rapidly. Months later, he actually died in that car, and the anger flared again. I had to sell an almost new car because I could not deal with even the sight of it.

I am not one to get angry, but occasionally something could get to me when Ron was dying. A minister friend of Ron's came to see him when he was on hospice, but he didn't come to his ash-scattering service, and I received no form of condolence from his church. I thought that was strange, but it was the least of my concerns at that point. A year later I met a very nice man, and as we were talking, I found out that he went to that minister's church. I found myself peeved and unable to carry on the conversation. Now, this poor man had nothing to do with what had happened, and as I reflected, I was embarrassed by my behavior. As I look at it now, I realize that it was my anger that bubbled up. I forgave myself, and hope I will be aware if something like that starts to happen again.

Kelly expressed it beautifully: "I never felt anger; I believe that learning that mourning is one of love's facets was key to my lack of anger. My girlfriend Charlene knew her time was coming. She did not shrink from life; indeed, she chose me for her final romance. Brave, calm, strong, she carried on and gave me an example that I remain awed by."

Bargaining: Bargaining occurs when you want to make a deal with a higher power that you will give anything for more time with your loved one. Bonnie said, "My husband died a year after a cancer diagnosis and there was never any denial. Bargaining happened for me—for both of us—while he was still alive, but not at all after his death for me." When, after a death, you find yourself wishing that you could go back and change something that would have prevented your loved one's departure, you are wanting to bargain, but it never works.

Jacques's best friend—actually he was the best man at our wedding—was visiting at our home after we had all attended a celebration. He died in a car accident on his way home. Receiving the devastating phone call an hour later made me spin with "if only" I had insisted he stay with us (I had and it didn't work), or "if only" we had encouraged him to not drink so much in the first place (we had), or if only I had given him more coffee (I had), but I still kept thinking I could have prevented his accident. Having "if only" thoughts is an indication of bargaining.

Bargaining happens especially in cases where the death is sudden, because we think there might have been a way to prevent it. But bargaining also comes up in relation to suffering. Bargaining with God can occur when someone says "if only" God will take pain away from our loved one, we will never miss attending church again. And when the pain only

gets worse, this may lead to a crisis of faith. Recognizing that
the bargaining you do will not change the ultimate outcome can
help you to see the futility of it so that you can shift to focusing
on what you can do.

Depression: The depression that occurs while grieving is
not a mental illness. Depression is perfectly normal in grief.
It may show up as sadness or loneliness, and you may or may
not realize that you have it. You may feel in a fog, or you may
feel intense sadness. You may isolate yourself and spend time
thinking of the past, leading to feelings of emptiness and
despair. This is a stage that will take as long as it takes. There
is no rushing depression, and if you do rush, you may just be
hiding or ignoring what you are experiencing. Many employers
give a brief bereavement leave and expect employees to "get
over it" and get back to their normal level of work as soon
as they return. If this is your situation, you may want to talk
to your supervisor, or you may want to just do your job and
deal with how you feel when you get home. This is a difficult
way to go.

Ellis experienced anger in dealing with his mother's health.
He was living halfway across the country when his brother
called him to come home right away because his mother
wasn't doing well. He arrived home to find his mother on
life support in ICU and discovered that she was on the brink
of having her leg, possibly both legs, amputated because of
complications of diabetes. His brothers had not shared with
him that she had diabetes. He and his brothers decided to take
her off life support, knowing then how severely her health was
compromised. He was depressed by the situation and angry
that he had to return home and deal with it on his own. Be sure
to take care of yourself during the process, and get help when
you need it.

Acceptance: When you realize that your loved one no longer has a physical presence in your life, then you have reached acceptance. This is the time when you start discovering your new normal. You develop new patterns that suit you. You meet new people. You reestablish connections with people you haven't had time to devote to. You try new things to see what works for you now and what doesn't, and you can make the choice of what serves you best. I started a new routine that includes meditation, journaling, going to the gym, writing, and creating in my studio. In the past, I wanted to do all these things, but I hadn't established patterns of doing them regularly because there were always things that needed to be tended to and emergencies arose. Now that I am on my own, I choose what is most important to me and focus on it. Some counselors add the concept of hope to this stage.

Carla shares this example of acceptance: "I was with my father when he said his last conscious words. He wanted to stand up, it was very important for him that he stand up. I told him he was too weak, but he begged me to help him stand up. I helped him sit up and put his arms over my shoulders and grabbed him around his waist. He breathed deep and said thank you and we just stood there for a few minutes. I laid him back down and he curled up and slept peacefully for a while. A little while later, the hospice nurse came to check on Dad and he was really restless. He started swinging his arms and cussing (my dad rarely cussed). We sat with him and soothed him. He died early the next morning. On a side note, I was reading *Love in the Time of Cholera* and, just after this incident, I read a scene in which one of the characters was dying and fighting off the angel of death in a similar fashion. Hospice brought in a hospital bed at this time and we helped transfer Dad to that bed, where he relaxed immediately into a peaceful sleep he never came out of. Later, I remembered the story and thought that Dad was fighting off the angel of death because he didn't want to die in the bed he had shared with Mom, because he was concerned for her feelings about sleeping in his death bed. That thought, true or not, really let me accept Dad's death as a part of the family dynamic."

Reconstruction is another stage that some counselors use. Life for you cannot stay the same as before the death of your loved one. Reconstruction refers to a period of putting things back together. You may have to find another place to live or to conduct a business you own, or your changes may involve remembering to do regular tasks that there is no one to help you with now, like taking out the trash. This is the time to work through what is different now, decide what needs to be changed and what doesn't, and then move forward.

An old school of thought stipulated that you had to go through each of the stages of grief to heal from grief. Nothing about that statement is true. If one of the stages resonates with you and you can gain peace by reflecting on it, by all means do, but no guidelines exist that state exactly what you need in exactly the correct order. And "healing" is not something that comes in relationship to grief.

Practice: Your Stages of Grief

Almost everybody goes through some of the stages. In your journal, explore experiences you have had with the stages listed in this chapter. Can you think of any other stages that weren't in the chapter? Did reading about these stages help you on your journey? Take your time with this. Don't rush through it, and you may want to come back to what you wrote when you think of other examples later on. Writing through the process of your loss is the best active thing to do to work your way back to the joy you have felt in the past. You can feel joy every day, and this is your goal that you can accomplish through all you are doing now.

Key Tips for Chapter 13

- Everyone will experience the stages that are relevant to them.

- There is no particular order of grief you must follow.

- Grief does not end when you finish going through stages, but it can transform into a place of love.

Chapter 14

Your Memories

"I'll be seeing you in all the old familiar places that
this heart of mine embraces all day through."

—Billie Holiday

Our love lasts forever in our hearts through the memories we
hold. What we remember most is usually generated from strong
emotions, the highest highs and lowest lows in our lives. The
key here is that we can choose what we remember and how
we keep our memories alive. What do you want to remember?
What would you like others to remember?

In Hawaii, we have a tradition called "talk story." The
tradition started as a way to pass on information, news, and
history, as the ancestors didn't have a way to write things down.
The Hawaiians love the tradition so much that it is still an
important part of Hawaiian culture. Children learn to talk story
in their classrooms, and it is always a treat to talk story with
Hawaiian kupunas, the elders. Talking story is a great way to
share memories. My dad told me the story of the first time his
father saw a train. They had been watching train tracks being
built, but no one really understood the concept of what a train

was. When the tracks were finished, people gathered to see the first train come into town. As the train got closer and closer, my grandfather got closer and closer to the ground! He felt the ground shaking as he was sitting on it when the train passed. For me, that story put into perspective how fast our society is surging forward. In my dad's lifetime, we went from trains to a man on the moon and more.

When we are grieving, talking story can bring joy and/ or tears. Many people avoid talking about someone who has died because either they don't want to bring pain to a loved one, or they can't handle the memories. If this is the case with the people around you and you want to talk, speak your loved one's name. Give people permission to share memories. Tell them it's okay. Talking to people when you can't speak the name of your loved one, or they can't bear to hear it, can be difficult, awkward, and exhausting. The part of your life spent with the person who died did not disappear, and ignoring it in conversation does not make it go away. Say what you need to say. Tell your truth the way you remember it.

I love the Jewish prayer that speaks to the importance of memories:

" 'We Remember Them' expresses the belief that the souls of our loved ones live on through those who remember them in all times and circumstances: When we are weary and in need of strength, we remember them... When we have joys we yearn to share, we remember them. By extending life to them in remembrance, we are free to live through and beyond our grief: 'As long as we live, they too shall live, for they are now a part of us, as we remember them.' "

Your memories represent your truth as you remember it. We all remember things differently and remember different things. I once witnessed a car accident. I was standing in a line waiting to get into a building. All who were in the line were facing the same direction and saw the same accident, but we each remembered things differently. I saw a child standing in the front seat before the car was struck by a truck. Someone else saw that child sitting in the backseat after the accident. A man noticed that the truck was speeding. Someone else noticed that the truck did not stop at the stop sign. We all witnessed the same thing, but each saw it differently. Don't be surprised, when you share memories, if they are not the same. We attended a friend's funeral where the friend's boss came up to us after the service to offer condolences. He said very nice things about our friend, which was the opposite of how he had treated our friend and what he had told other people. I was proud of my daughter when she called him on it, but I am not sure he actually realized what he was saying. He was saying what he thought he should under the circumstances, instead of speaking his truth.

When we don't share memories, either by speaking them or writing them, the memories can fade away. Take some time to consider what is important to you to remember about your loved one and how you can keep that memory alive. My husband Ron had been estranged from his son through most of his son's adulthood. Though he wanted a relationship with his son, it hadn't happened. He would occasionally reach out, and finally his son agreed to see him. We had a wonderful visit. They both realized how much they had missed and started staying more in touch. When his son discovered that he was going to become a father, he asked my husband if he would write his story so that he would be able to tell his son about his grandfather, and I think he wanted to learn about his father, too. My husband wanted to tell his story rather than write it, but he died before he could. I had only known my husband for the last ten years of his life, and his life was rich and full before me. And, while he knew me, he chose to live in the present, so there was much I didn't learn about his life. After he died, I decided to write what I could remember of the stories he told me of his life. I also shared the stories with his daughter. I do regret that I didn't start this project while he was still here to help me fill in the blanks.

Not all memories are good, especially if your loved one died in tragic circumstances or if you had important things left unsaid or undone. This happens often, and if it is your situation, you will need to deal with it. When you try to protect yourself from certain memories, they may become worse and be detrimental to you. You may want to try writing about these memories, talking to a trusted friend, or getting professional counseling. Most of all, take care of you right now. You are here, now, and you are precious.

Talking and writing about how you first met your loved one can spark special memories that warm your heart. I met Jacques at a party. I loved his smile and humor right away, which led to a great friendship long before romance entered the picture. Though Ron and I said we met online, we remembered after we had dated a while that we had actually met at the university, where we both attended a lecture. I remember his warm handshake and my thinking that I'd love to get to know him, and then I did! Jeanette told me about when she met her husband: "I formally met my husband when I was interviewing him for the opening of his exhibit at the art museum. I had a little good-news TV show that aired in the mornings. I had seen him at the museum and at a few events but hadn't really had the opportunity to spend much time getting to know him. I found myself enchanted by his work and how he spoke of his creations. Years later, when we watched the show together, I was obviously smitten, and he was flirting himself; we got quite a laugh over that. I wondered how many viewers saw how much we were acting like teenagers." Bonnie said that her first memory of her husband was: "When he was introduced at a writing group at a bookstore. He looked more like a lumberjack than a writer."

I ask people what their favorite memories are of their loved one, and their answer often leads to beautiful conversations. Sherry said: "I was married for forty-seven years to my Darling John. He had the biggest heart I'd ever known. He helped me to find confidence and courage in myself which I so lacked. He believed in me so strongly, that I finally found, and came to appreciate, my self-worth. He wrote me a love note almost every day of our lives together and always called me his 'Angel Girl.' This great love carried over to his daughter, son, their spouses, and their children." Ellis told me: "When my mom was in hospice, I played Sam Cooke because she loved his voice. I wanted her to hear a great songbird while she was still here on this earth. When my mom passed on, I saw her spirit go on as well, and what a wonderful sight to see!" Bonnie told me that a favorite memory of hers was the last wedding anniversary they were able to really celebrate. "We drove to a huge sliding board in a town in Maryland. We slid down together, hand-in-hand, shouting out our love for one another, landing in a big heap, me on top of him. We laughed for what seemed like hours." I can't help but smile when I think about their joy!

Karyn shared her favorite memory. "My favorite time with Jim was every day. To be special, it was our trip to Italy with my brother Bruce and his lady love Suzie. It came at the end of Jim's life, at a point where every smile or glance was magic. As time drew closer to his leaving, we cherished every breath." I feel their love in her words.

Carla's favorite memory was, "The first time my family invited my boyfriend Glenn (now my husband) out to dinner, I believe we were at Mexicali restaurant. My dad looked seriously at Glenn and told him to 'eat every bean and pea in your plate.'

Glenn looked at him bewildered, wondering about my family, I'm sure, because he heard 'eat every bean, and pee in your plate.' Then Dad started laughing and we explained the joke. Dad loved to tell stories that sounded believable until the end, when it got ridiculous. I loved to see people's reactions to the stories."

Another way to remember your loved one is to share what you think he or she would want to be remembered for. I know Ron would love to be remembered as a spiritual man who loved to inspire others with his creativity. Businesses and relationships were started or greatly improved by his advice. Bonnie said of her husband: "Gil would like to be remembered for two things: One, standing up for what he believed in. Two, the importance of being the best friend possible—being the one anyone could call at three in the morning for anything at all. These are the two things I would also like him to be remembered for." Jeanette said her husband would want to be remembered, "As an artist. I loved that about him. We shared our love of the arts. It was our glue." Karyn said: "Jim is remembered by all that knew him as a special, deeply gentle man."

Carla wrote this long memory of what her dad would want to be remembered for. I love how she put her memories in writing: "Dad cared for family more than anything. When he was older, he always said he didn't want any presents, he just wanted us there to share the celebration. Dad was raised by his grandmother after his mother tried to give him and his brother away. He adored his grandmother. She walked them out of Mexico during the Mexican Revolution and worked cleaning offices to take care of them. Dad started working for Western Union as a messenger boy when he was sixteen, and said he went to school in his uniform so he could go right to work. He had to help support the family. When we were kids, Dad visited his younger brother George a couple of times a year. We would usually visit as a family. It took me years to understand that Uncle George and his roommate and friend Jack were a couple. Dad said once he didn't like his brother being gay and even threatened him at one time when he brought a guy home when they were kids, but his grandmother, who raised them, stopped the fight and reinforced 'Family first!' Dad always treated his brother and his friends respectfully and, when George was dying, Dad acknowledged Jack as the person who made the decisions for George's care and the disposition of his property at a time when that wasn't a given. Losses had underlined the value he placed on us (Mom, Paul and I). My oldest brother David died in a car accident when he was eighteen. I was nine, and it was devastating to the family. My next oldest brother George died of cancer at fifty-three. George was six years older than I was. Dad said a parent shouldn't have to see their child die. George had left home at eighteen, was in the Navy for four years, came back home for a few months, and left again for Oregon. He spent most of his life away from Mom and Dad... My brother Paul (one year older) and I were almost a second family, and experienced our parents differently. Dad had more problems accepting Paul going to college to be a musician than he did accepting me, a girl, going to college. He was very afraid that Paul would be penniless and without a means to support himself, and worried about how Paul was doing in his later years... I didn't appreciate how unusual it was for a Mexican man to support higher education for his daughter until I was a teacher and saw over and over again students whose parents didn't want them to go to college because they needed to stay home and take care of the family... He loved Mom, who was always his 'favorite blonde,' and he loved to tease her. Mom says he could be difficult, but they were a generation that kept it together, and we saw more working together than anything else. Dad was very active in church and veteran's groups. He and Mom worked with most of the groups together. In the '70s, they were both involved with the Bakersfield Community Theater: Dad helped with the theater remodel and Mom did costumes. In the '80s they were very involved in the Kern County Museum's Historical Society. He would love to be remembered for making a contribution to his community and raising his family. He was proud of who he was, what he came from, and successfully feeding, sheltering, and raising his family. We didn't have a lot of extras and my brother and I had to pay for our own college, but Dad and Mom worked together to make sure we had a home."

What can you do to keep your memories? My parents kept many boxes full of memories, most of which weren't relevant to me. When you consider what to do, think about what you want to remember and how you best can preserve and/or share those memories. Here are some ideas:

- When my grandfather died, my father gave me his armoire. Though it was old and somewhat dilapidated, Grandpa had stored all of his belongings in it, and it was a treasure to me. Is there something that belonged to your loved one that you can keep as a treasure or that would be a treasure to a family member or friend?

- Jason, my son, got a tattoo which represented my husband to him. Every time he notices it, he thinks of Jacques, and he will always have it with him.

- My grandmother had been the cook for the school her children attended. My mother kept the recipes Grandma had written out by hand in her favorite cookbook. When my mother died, that book and those recipes, including my mom's recipes which

I discovered she had written there, became a treasure to me.

- For Ron's memorial service, his daughter Saffronia made a beautiful video collage of his life. The family were all able to get a copy to keep remembering him by.

- I made a photo collage of my grandparents and parents that hangs in my office so that I can remember them every day.

- At Christmas, I have special ornaments I put on the tree that bring memories of friends and family. I even have a tiny Christmas stocking my mother gave me when I was pregnant the first time. Even though that baby didn't make it through the pregnancy, every year I remember all the love I had.

- My dear friend Rose has a collection of art I have created over the years. Whenever I visit her home, I know I won't be forgotten.

- When Ron died, people shared memories on Facebook and Instagram. These memories can reach many people.

- When Ron and I were dating, he came to help me plant some flowers, and he brought his grandmother's trowel with him. I was so touched by how he saved that and that it was still important to him because of the memories he shared with her.

- Jacques and I invested in bricks with our names on them for a plaza in our hometown. I thought people would remember us when they saw those bricks for a long time.

- Karyn said: "My first memory of Jim was of a beautiful trim man with a tennis racket in his hand who wandered into my antique store early one morning. I was playing whale songs and he thought they were beautiful. We connected with our eyes, but he left to have his tennis racket restrung at a shop in the back of our center. We didn't meet again for several years, until we both attended a social event at the beach. He was attracted to me like a magnet. Unfortunately, I was in the midst of a divorce, and he walked away when I told him. A year later, at my new house, I gave a breakfast for all of the single people that I knew. After brunch, we went bowling and Jim was on my team. I couldn't stop looking at him and his lovely legs. He was in tennis shorts, having come from playing tennis. We were smitten. After bowling, everyone came back to my house for lunch and games. Everyone stayed, enjoying the view and the nice group of people. Jim never left my side, and we were together for twenty-two wonderful years thereafter."

Think about ways you can remember your loved one. Remember their love, their gifts, their talents, their service, their integrity, their actions, their humor. Only you can control your memories of your loved one. Grief experts seem to agree that remembering loved ones is essential for healing in the process of your transformation. And people who have a way of keeping their memories alive fare better than those who don't. You are the only one responsible for your memories, so remember what is most important to you. Memories are a constant reminder of the gift of love you have been given, which will never go away.

Practice: Talk Story

What would you want someone to remember about you? Now is your chance to write your story. And you can write more than one, but start with a favorite memory you have that you would love to be remembered for. When you are choosing what to write, pick something that shows the real you, not just something you accomplished. My head is full of interesting and/or entertaining stories that I would love to share, but I need to write them one at a time. Start by making a list of your very favorite stories. Then prioritize what you would like to write. When you choose one story, first write a list of all the details you want to be sure to include. Then, string your details together into your finished product.

Wonderful inspiration for this style of writing can be found in the short book *The Last Lecture*, by Randy Pausch. I highly recommend this book, which was written after Pausch received a diagnosis of terminal cancer and is about seizing the moment, my favorite concept.

Key Tips for Chapter 14

- Remembering good times and experiences can bring you joy.
- The importance of sharing memories with friends and relatives.
- How writing memories helps you grieve.

Chapter 15

What Others Say

" 'I'm sorry for your loss': the *aloha* of condolences."
—Laurie Kilmartin

When someone dies, people have a tendency to feel they need to say something to address what happened, so they will something useless, like, "I'm sorry for your loss," then skip right over to the next thing that they want to say, like "When are you coming back to work?" or "How about those Dodgers?" I got to the point where, when someone said "I'm sorry for your loss," I could barely be civil, so I generally didn't respond at all. Were they comparing my tragedy to losing their car keys? I wanted to say, "I didn't lose my husband. He died." And at the same time, I knew they were doing the best they could. That feeble phrase is probably the condolence most often offered. What does this mean to you?

You have the opportunity to respond to what someone says to you about your situation in ways that can help you and that may even help the person speaking to you. Generally, when someone says something to you about the death of your loved one, they do care. They don't mean to be hurtful. They may just be repeating something they heard someone else say because they just don't know how to express what they are feeling. Let's look at some of the common things people say to someone who is grieving and explore ways you can respond.

"I'm sorry for your loss." Instead of just saying thank you, try saying something like "I know your friendship meant the world to him," or "I am sure you are hurting, too." This kind of response can lead to a conversation that can help both of you to ease the pain and have a deeper understanding of each other. And sometimes, "Thank you" may be all you can say, and that's okay.

"How are you doing?" The person who says this may think they want to know the real answer to this, but chances are they don't. If you respond with "Fine" or "Okay," generally they will go on to talk about something else. People said this to me a lot, and I always responded, "The best I can." That was the truth for me at that moment. What could have been more helpful is to be more specific. You could say something like, "I am feeling better than I was, but I would love to spend some time with you to just talk." This would open an opportunity for you both.

"Let me know if there is anything I can do for you." People usually would like to help, but don't know what to do. Instead of answering, "Okay, I will," try asking for something that would really help right then, like asking them to get some stamps for thank-you notes from the post office for you. Or ask for some help with childcare so you can have some time for yourself. Or ask them to go to lunch with you because you aren't comfortable going out alone right now. Think of something that would really help you, or something that could benefit you both.

"He brought this on himself." People really do say this, especially in cases like lung cancer after a lifetime of smoking. Or amputations leading to death for an obese diabetic. Or death in a car accident for a person known to drink and drive. First, forgive the person who said something like this, because carrying around anger at them does not help you or them. The response to this person can be challenging. You could say something like, "I not sure why you would say that to me at this time, and I know you will understand that I can't talk to you right now." Or "You must be hurting right now."

"You are so strong in dealing with her death." Sometimes people say what they want to see instead of what is real. Maybe you do look strong to others because you put your game face on and don't talk about your feelings, but when someone says something like this, think about how you must be appearing to those around you. Maybe looking strong is all you can do to keep from breaking into sobs. And that's okay. To respond to someone who says this, you could say something like, "Looks are deceiving. I really am having a hard time, but I am doing the best I can when I am in public." A statement like this can lead to a deeper conversation or support. Or you may want to say something like, "Thank you for noticing. I actually do feel stronger than I thought I would, but it's still hard. I'd love to talk to you about it sometime."

"Time heals all wounds." True, time passes, and you probably dwell less on your loved one as time goes by, but you will always carry some bereavement in your heart. You could say something like, "I can see why you would say that, but I don't believe in healing from grief. I will always remember the love we shared, and that brings me comfort." Or "I am sure as time passes, I will be spending less time dwelling with my loss, but I can't say I will heal from it. What do you think?"

"You can always have another baby." You know that one life does not replace another, and you are hurting now. This kind of statement is not constructive, but again, you must consider the source. This person just didn't know what to say. You could respond with "I know that, but I will always miss my precious baby." Or "Let me tell you about Matthew. He was such a sweet baby."

"You go to the grave too much." My mother-in-law went to her husband's grave every birthday, every holiday, and every time she wanted to in between. That was how she dealt with her feelings, and it worked for her. She was always so happy when she got to go visit. While I prefer not to go to cemeteries, I respect the choice of the person dealing with the death of their loved one. You could say, "That might not be what you would choose, but it works for me." Or "Would you like to go with me the next time I go? I feel so much peace there."

"You can always get married again." Falling in love with someone else right now is probably the last thing on your mind, and you certainly don't need someone to suggest getting married right now. While ultimately being open to what the rest of your life offers you, right now, taking it one step at a time may be what's best for you. You could say, "I'm not ready to think about that right now." Or "Hold that thought! Don't need it right now, but I do appreciate you thinking of me."

"He's in a better place now." This is such a loaded statement. Better than your arms? Better than your home? Better than with your family? And the person who says something like this may have entirely different beliefs than you do. In response to this, you could say, "I'm not quite sure what you mean by 'better place.' I just know that I miss him right now." Or "I am glad that thought brings you peace."

"I know just how you feel." People tend to say something like this if they have had someone they love die. Every experience of the death of a loved one is different, so the chances that someone knows how someone else actually feels are not high. A person who says this is probably reliving their own pain and just wants to help. You could say, "Tell me about your experience," or "We have something in common. Let's talk about it sometime."

You have to let your emotions out. First, you don't have to do anything. Each person responds in different ways to a death, and so many factors go into that response. If a person was ill and suffering for a long time, the emotion may be joy or relief instead of tears. If the person died of suicide or murder or an accident, you may be in shock and not appear to be grieving at all. A statement like this is a reflection of the belief of the person saying it. Know that you just need to do what you feel like doing, what helps you. You could say, "Thank you for your concern. I am handling my situation in my own way." Or "I do let my emotions out, just not where anyone else can see. That's what works for me."

"I don't know what to say." Or they say nothing. They may just have no idea what to say. Sometimes silence is the very best they can do. When that is the case, you can choose to be silent with them. That can be a soothing, peaceful experience. Or you can choose to speak first to them. You could say, "Come sit with me and hold my hand." Or "Would you like to talk?" The key here is not to mistake not talking for not caring.

With each of these statements, I felt like typing "Really?" after I wrote it. Yes, people really do say these things, as appalling as some of them are. Your feelings are your own, and people will try to help by giving all kinds of advice. Use what serves you and ignore the rest. Your responsibility is not to console them, but responding to their thoughts may lead you to a healing conversation for you both.

I heard that a friend of mine was asking about me because she was concerned that I wasn't doing well since she had seen me posting things about grief and grieving on Facebook and Instagram. I realized that she wasn't able to ask me personally how I was because she didn't know what to say, so I reached out to her. Fortunately, I was at a place that I could do that, but that would not always have been the case. It's like the safety instructions on an airplane—put the oxygen mask on your face first. Then, when you are breathing, you can help someone else.

You will hear others say positive and negative things about you, your marriage, your life. Don't be shaped by what they say. I used to love to read the reviews of plays I performed in until someone told me that, if I believed the positive things the reviewer said about my performance, I had to believe the negative things too. I stopped reading the reviews and continued to give my very best performance every time.

So, you don't have to believe what others say. Live in your truth. Do, be, and say your own thing. That's what counts!

Practice: Affirmations

This chapter is about what others say to us. Affirmations are what we say to ourselves. Writing and saying affirmations is a method to recognize who we are and what is most important to us. When you write an affirmation, always start with the words "I am." These powerful words affirm the truth of what you are saying. Write who you are right now, or who you are stepping into being. I write affirmations like:

- I am strong and healthy.

- I am guided and inspired.

- I am whole, complete, and perfect.

Speaking these words and believing them guide you into being the person you describe. I write affirmations in my journal every day to remind me of who I truly am. Or who I truly want to be. For instance, if you are feeling weak and desire to pull yourself together and move forward, you could write "I am strong." Then believe that about yourself and step into that strength. Look at all you have just been through. You are still here, in one piece. That takes strength, so you are strong. Your intention will remind you of that.

Now write three intentions that are just for you. What do you need to be most at this moment? What do you know about yourself that you would like to be better? Who would you like to be now, that you hadn't thought about being before? Who would your ideal self be? What affirmations would you write to express any of these things? I had some health challenges when I was grieving. In my case, I knew I wasn't seriously ill, but I did feel lousy. I needed to just feel better, so a frequent affirmation of mine was, and is, "I am whole, complete, and perfect." I also had a tendency to not do things because I would tell myself I was too tired. When I recognized that, my affirmation would be, "I am full of energy and can do anything I desire!" When you say your affirmations often enough, you will find yourself believing in them. Try writing at least one affirmation every day, based on how you really want to be or feel. Then say your affirmations to yourself to yourself often. And it's okay to repeat affirmations to remind yourself of who you are.

Key Tips for Chapter 15

- Common phrases like "I am sorry for your loss" are not helpful.

- Ways to respond to people when they are trying to express sympathy.

- Ways to take care of yourself when people unknowingly say hurtful things.

Chapter 16

Grief Is Healthy

"Where I am, let me be present."

—Ricki Byars

Grief is a healthy response. Being sad and remembering things you don't want to can bring up tears and heartache, but things have to come up to help you heal. Some days the weight is so heavy you have to just lie down alone, and if that's the case, just do it. Sometimes you want to read a book or watch a movie. If that's the case, just do it. Know, though, that avoiding your feelings will only make them harder to deal with. Grieve for as little or as much time as you need. Only you know the answer to that.

Loss and stress really do affect your health. In a study done by Rice University, they discovered that "people who struggle to overcome grief caused by loss of a loved one are at greater risk of suffering from potentially deadly levels of inflammation. Conversely, those who have an easier time dealing with a spouse's death are prone to healthier outcomes." We have all heard of couples who have been together for many years who die within hours or days of each other. This is caused by real, physical symptoms that can arise because they truly just cannot live without their loved one. If you have physical symptoms you are concerned about, be sure to seek medical attention. And take time to evaluate your loss. Where are you in your loss right now? What steps can you take to help?

When someone avoids going through the process of grief, they can stay tied to the past, and as much as you may think you would like to, that's just not possible. Yet it is not unusual to unconsciously try to stay the same. Though you don't stop being a mother, a wife, a son, a husband, a daughter, a granddaughter, a grandmother, a friend, a partner, or whatever role you played before someone died, now is when you need to shift gears into the main role you are playing now. And you can start by recognizing any symptoms of grief you may be dealing with. And developing a plan to actively help yourself.

Get out a journal or notebook and write out your answers to these questions. After you do, we'll talk about each one.

What do you do to keep yourself healthy now?

- I eat well ____
- I spend time with friends and family ____
- I exercise to stay fit ____
- I smile and do things that make me happy ____
- I spend time finding things that inspire me ____
- I am clear about my life's meaning ____
- I have a healthy balance between time I spend grieving and my everyday life ____
- I look forward to tomorrow and my future ____

What would you like to start to help you to be healthy?

- I'd like to eat better ____
- I'd like to spend more time with people ____

- I'd like to improve my exercise practice _____
- I'd like to have a reason to smile _____
- I'd like to be inspired _____
- I'd like to discover the meaning of life _____
- I'd like to do something besides grieve _____
- I'd like to be able to look past today _____

Answering these questions will give you a good idea of how you are doing right now. Some of your answers may be in between what you are doing now and what you'd like to do, and as with everything, we always have room for improvement. Let's explore what you can do right now to help with your transformation.

I'd Like to Eat Better

To eat better, look at how you are eating now. Although traditional nutrition says you should eat breakfast, lunch, and dinner, that may not work for you. What is more important is what you eat and how much you eat. Early on, I found it difficult to eat at all and would just heat up some frozen vegetables or make some instant mashed potatoes if I felt hungry. This wasn't very balanced and did little to build up my strength. I have known others who tried to feel better by constant snacking. This also wasn't balanced and led to less energy by always feeling over-full. The key here is balance and food choices. For me, cutting out processed food helped me feel better both physically and emotionally. I knew eating this way was a choice that had no negatives and could only help me.

Try planning what you will be eating. Choose something easy to have for breakfast. Having the same thing every day, or a variation of that thing, eliminates having to put too much time and energy into preparation. Try having something like oatmeal, which can be varied by adding a variety of fruits, nuts, and seasonings, like cinnamon. Or try avocado toast, which is so easy to make. I just make a piece of toast with hearty bread, mash half a ripe avocado onto it, add a little Sriracha sauce and salt flakes. Yum! You can change it by adding any seasonings you'd like along with a little sliced tomato, nuts, seeds, or even fruit.

For lunch, try full-fat Greek yogurt, which can be combined with fresh fruit or vegetables and anything else you'd like to add. They key is to find something you really like, keep it on hand, and be sure to eat it. Keep dinners simple, too. Making something you can divide up to eat for several meals helps save time, and you don't have to worry about coming up with something different to eat all the time. I do things like making a batch of chili and freezing it in individual servings, then serving it with a salad for a nice meal. Or I fix a batch of marinara sauce that I can freeze portions of so all I have to do is cook some pasta and fix a vegetable or salad to go with it. The key is to eat nutritious, unprocessed food, and eat it regularly.

Keep a variety of healthy snacks on hand, like celery and peanut butter, or a trail mix with nuts, seeds, and dried fruit. The key with snacks is to eat a reasonable-sized portion. You don't want to kill your appetite for your next meal. And only keep healthy snacks on hand. If you buy a big bag of chips or cookies, you probably will eat them all, and that doesn't serve you. And have dessert occasionally, too. A little something sweet can be so comforting. And again, just use thoughtful portion control. If you buy a whole cake, you may eat it, so try buying a beautiful little cupcake from a bakery instead and savor it.

The key to healthy eating is to be mindful. Only eat food that will serve your heart and your body, and only eat portions of a size that will provide adequate nutrition without excess calories.

I'd Like to Spend More Time with People

I used to say I wanted to spend time with people from my seat on the couch, and the people didn't come. The key here is to get off the couch! When we sit alone most of the time, we can easily slip into sadness and thinking about all we don't have. This doesn't serve us. But what about if you feel abandoned? Your friends have all gone on with their lives and here you sit. I remember when sitting was the best I could do. But, eventually, I had to get up.

Think about who you would really like to spend some time with. And think about what you would like that time to look like. I didn't know too many people on the island where I live, so I thought about who of the people I had met I would like to get to know better. One person I called said she was busy, but that she did like to take time to walk on the beach and asked if I'd like to come along. She was a regular beach walker, so I was amazed that I did keep up with her. Getting outside in the fresh air felt so good, and having a conversation with someone about something other than my loss was just what I needed. I called another friend and she suggested we do something different. She asked me what I hadn't done yet on the island that I would really like to do. I immediately thought of a botanical garden I had heard about, so we went there together. The garden was full of tropical plants and flowers that had all been planted by the owners years ago, and even had two big, beautiful natural waterfalls. Now I think about who I would like to spend time with or get to know better, and I think of something I'd like to do or someplace I'd like to go. I make a phone call or send

an email, then I get off my couch. It feels wonderful, and I
am grateful.

I'd Like to Improve My Exercise Practice

If you haven't been moving much, starting slow is a good idea.
Before you get out of bed, try pulling your knees up to your
chest and hold them there for a nice stretch. When you get
up, stand nice and straight and look up. Reach your hands
out toward the ceiling and take a nice, deep breath. Just these
two simple things will help you wake up and add a nice start
to your day.

When I lived on the mainland, I went to the gym and I did
water aerobics regularly. When we got to Maui, I found that,
due to his health, I needed to stay close by Ron, so I eventually
got out of the habit of exercising at all. After he died, it took
months before I got around at all, and as they say, if you don't
use it, you lose it. I couldn't even walk in a store. I had to use a
little cart I could ride in. I knew I was way too young for that,
and I wanted to do better. First, I went to the doctor, who saw
that my high blood pressure had come down to be low, so he
took me off my blood pressure medicine, and that made a huge
difference in my energy level. Sometimes, when our stress
levels change, our physical health changes too, so if your health
seems to be different than you expect it to be, get it checked
out. I felt like a whole new person when I didn't have to take
that medicine anymore.

When my health insurance started coverage for gym
membership, I joined and signed up with a trainer. I was so out
of shape I could hardly do anything, and I was determined to
get better. It took months of slow progress, but now I am better
every time I go. My muscle strength has returned, I breathe
easier, and I go on regular walks, enjoying the beauty of where

I live. So even if it is hard, even if you have never exercised, you can do better than you are right now, and trust me, it's worth it.

I'd Like to Have a Reason to Smile

Getting in the habit of not smiling is an easy trap to fall into. You may feel there is nothing to smile about and nothing makes you happy. I understand. I have been there. And it seems that the feeling will be eternal, but it doesn't have to be. Learning to smile again may take a while, and you can do it. Try getting out your journal. If you have written a journal in the past, read through it and find things you wrote when you were happy. Where were you? Who were you with? Do you discover things you could do, places you could go, or people you could be with where you were happy in the past? If you didn't write experiences like this, then take some time to contemplate things that have brought you joy in the past, even if it was long ago.

I used to spend lots of time sewing, quilting, and crocheting. When I was going through boxes in my house, I found a quilt that my grandmother had made me that was falling apart. Putting it back together is a big job, and I decided to fix it by hand. When I spend evenings hand-sewing and quilting while watching television, I don't feel nearly as alone as I had been. I remember my grandma's love and hugs, and even if I don't have a big smile, I feel better.

Spend some time looking in your mirror. I usually only look when I am combing my hair, but go beyond that. Really look at yourself. How do you look? Practice smiling. See all the different ways you can smile. Do a Mona Lisa smile, then try a smile like you would do as a child when someone tickled you. See how beautiful you are? There's nothing I like better than a toddler's laugh. You can see the joy in their whole bodies. Just watching them feels good, and you just naturally smile or laugh along with them.

Another way to get inspired is to watch YouTube. Search something like "funny animals" or "things that make you laugh." I just searched that, and I found myself laughing out loud at the funny things animals and people do. When Jacques was ill, he loved watching *America's Funniest Home Videos* on television, and while I didn't always find them amusing, I couldn't help but laugh along with Jacques as we watched. I've also started recording some of the late-night shows like Stephen Colbert's just to watch the opening monologues which are current, topical, and usually hilarious. I even started watching *Saturday Night Live*. Watching things like this can get you started smiling and even laughing again, if you just relax into what you are watching and don't think about anything else. Just have fun.

I'd Like to Be Inspired

To be inspired, think about what inspires you. I just have to look around me to be encouraged and energized by what I see. Each morning, I go outside and listen to the birds and watch the butterflies. They all live free and do exactly what they need to without being told. Their inherent nature guides them to live their best lives, and yours can too! What do you do naturally without having to think about it? Take some time to appreciate what you already do, you enjoy, and you do well. Maybe that's cooking, or staying in touch with a special friend, or remembering birthdays. Maybe that's painting a picture or painting a house. Maybe that's reading a book that inspires you or writing a book that inspires others. Maybe you are already inspired, but your inspiration has been dampened by your lack of energy. If that's the case, recognizing that is the first step. The next step is to act on your inspiration.

Inspiration can come from anywhere. I was inspired by Jeanette, whose husband died not long before Jacques. Watching how she dealt with her life was motivating for me. She told me that she had been writing her morning pages every day, which she read about in the book *The Artist's Way* by Julia Cameron. Cameron suggests that, to be centered and inspired, you should start the day by writing out by hand whatever comes to your mind for three pages. So I did that and was amazed at what I discovered, from things I needed to deal with to things I was ready to create. I also saw Jeanette around people. She didn't always stay stuck at home like I did, and when I saw her, I couldn't help but smile back at her beautiful smile. And she invited me out to places I couldn't have let myself go alone at that point. Because she inspired me, I reach out to others now who are dealing with loss. So, who inspires you? What can you do based on that person's actions?

After Ron died, I felt I was floating, lacking the anchor of inspiration to do anything. I kept thinking that I didn't know what to do next. Then, when my friend Chappy died, I was inspired to help his wife Lori cope with this unexpected shock in her life. That led me to write a letter, which led me to create cards to send to her every week for a year, which led me to writing this book. Paying attention to that inspiration when it came out of the blue gave me the opportunity to pull myself up and help others in the process. And I am grateful.

I'd Like to Discover the Meaning of Life

In 1969, Peggy Lee released the song "Is That all There Is?" That song haunted me for years. Whenever a major event occurred in my life, the chorus of that song would run through my mind.

> "Is that all there is?
> Is that all there is?
> If that's all there is, my friend,
> Then let's keep dancing
> Let's get out the booze and have a ball
> If that's all there is."

The words led me to believe that I was missing something, that there had to be more to life than the pain I was feeling from experiences. When a loved one dies, questioning the meaning of life is a natural reaction. But what do you do about it?

Now is a good time for you to explore how you feel about your life experience. What are your beliefs? What brings you comfort? When Randy Pausch learned that he had terminal cancer, he wrote a book called *The Last Lecture*, where he summed up everything he believed about the life he led and what mattered most. His book became a phenomenon which swept the country. Reading it helped me look at my own life, how I had lived it, and what I wanted to be remembered for. With those points in mind, what would you write about you? Only you know the meaning of your life.

I'd Like to Do Something Different

If you'd like to do something besides worrying about your loss, think of the Nike motto: "Just do it." When you say something like "I'd like to," "I want to," or "I should," what you are really saying is "It's not going to happen." Try reframing your thoughts by starting your sentence with "I am." For instance, "I am walking on the beach today," or "I am baking cookies to take to my friend," or "I am inviting people to Thanksgiving dinner who don't have loved ones living nearby."

What have you always wanted to do? The concept of a "bucket list" has been popular, where you make a list of things you want to do before you die, and you could do that. But you may want to start with just one thing at a time. Right now, what is one thing you have frequently thought about doing but never did? This could be anything from going to a certain restaurant, to reading a special book, to taking dance lessons, to reconnecting with an old friend, to running in a marathon, to going to a concert. Choose one thing that is doable right now.

I always wanted to go to Tuscany. I know, that's a big one. But when I saw a trip to Tuscany come up for an organization I belong to, I decided it was time. Taking this trip was the most important thing I did to get my life back on track. I met great new people. I walked for miles. I saw incredible works of art I had studied about throughout my life. I ate great food. Most of all, I did it. And I came home a new person. I have more energy. I feel better. I get out more. I am moving forward with my life.

You don't need to go on a big trip or spend lots of money. You can start by choosing just one thing. Then, just do it!

I'd Like to Be Able to Look Past Today

When a loved one dies, our tomorrows will never look like we thought they would. Everything is different. The key is to learn to be okay with that. What helped me the most is committing to live in the moment. Right now, in this moment, I am happy, all my needs are met, and life is good. And every moment can be that way. Living in the moment is not failing to consider your future, but it is letting go of worry and fear. You can plan to move to a different house, get a different job, or join the gym. Plans are great and necessary, but you can't live in the future, or the past. You can remember the great times you had with your loved one, but you can't relive those times, just as you can't live tomorrow today. When you consider all that, you see that all you have is right now. And that is good. You can smile in this moment, smile at a memory of the past or a dream of the future, but choose to experience the present, right now. I do, and I am grateful.

Practice: Make a Plan

This chapter is full of inspiration for things to do. Take some time now to make a list of at least one thing in each category the chapter covers. Take your time with this and add to it as you think of things. When you are happy with your list, choose the one thing you would like to do the most, then do it.

After you do it, write in your journal about the experience. What did you enjoy about it? Did it inspire you to do more of what you did or inspire you to do something different? If it did, add this to your list. Then review your list and decide what the next thing is that you want to do. Just work on one thing at a time so that you can fully appreciate it. Some of the things, like stopping eating processed foods, will be something you can just incorporate into your life to do every day now. Others will be unique, one-time experiences that you can appreciate, then try something else. The point of using this list is to find ways to best enjoy your life and take care of yourself. Have a wonderful time!

Key Tips for Chapter 16

- Avoiding grief only makes it worse.
- Everyone grieves differently.
- Grieve as much or as little as you need to.

Chapter 17

Tell Your Story

"No experience is ever wasted."

—Oprah Winfrey

Grief and mourning are different. Grief is the normal response we have after someone dies. Mourning is your expression of grief. How people experience mourning is as different as people are, and mourning is essential to help us transform our grief. A large part of mourning is telling the story of our loss. Sometimes we will know someone to tell it to. Sometimes we will tell a stranger. And there are so many stories to tell. But in our culture, we often apologize for what we are feeling, like when tears come, embarrassing you, at a restaurant when your loved one's favorite food is served. We don't want to spoil everyone's time dining out, and we don't want to fall into that pit of despair where we don't feel comfortable expressing what is going on with us. So, what can we do?

Discovering the healthy way of mourning by telling your story is imperative to your transformation. Your story allows you to explore your memories however you want to. I found that, the more I told my stories, the less I needed to. I was able to wade through my sadness to a point where I could see things to be happy about. When I started going to the gym, my muscles would get so sore. Each step the next day reminded me of my pain, yet the more often I went, the better I felt, and if I did exercise to the point of pain, the pain was never as bad and didn't last as long. Mourning works much the same way through telling stories.

Prudential Insurance did a beautiful project online about dealing with mourning through memories by interviewing someone who was grieving and commissioning an artist to use that story to create a work of art. The person grieving then had a lovely artwork to look at and smile. Amelia, who was interviewed for this project, expressed that she was holding on hard to her memories till she realized that she could have those memories and then let them go. This didn't mean that the memories would go away or that she would love her husband who had died any less, but now she was able to not constantly dwell in her sorrow and move on to accept his passing. Check out the Masterpiece of Love project by Prudential online.

When a loved one dies, feeling like you are the only one suffering the pain that happens is not unusual. Pain after loss is normal and needs to be experienced. Telling your story about your pain can help you put everything in perspective. Listening to the stories of other people's loss can inspire us. Take Sheryl Sandburg, Chief Operating Officer for Facebook, for instance. Her husband died suddenly, unexpectedly leaving her with two young children. Her loss was difficult, and she made her experience public by writing the book *Option B*. The theory of *Option B* was that, when her first option didn't work the way everyone expected, her life and the lives of her children didn't stop, so she worked to discover her next best option to get on with her life. By writing that book, not only was she able to start working through her own loss, she also was able to bring comfort to others through the book and her huge community on Facebook, where people share their stories in the Option B Support Group: Coping with Grief. She also has a website where you can read the stories of others and find ways to build resilience.

What Stories Do You Need to Tell?

So many stories surround the loss of a loved one. The story you need to tell will be what matters to you most. Some stories are so deep and painful that you feel that you could never tell them. You don't have to tell those stories out loud. Write them down in a journal or on your computer. Then write them again. Each time, the story will change a little. Maybe this time you remember details that you forgot when you wrote it before. Or maybe this time you discover that you don't need to write as much detail. The more you tell the story, the easier it gets, whether you are telling your story to a close friend or family member or writing your story in your journal you lock away where no one can see. The key here is to just tell it.

Some idea for stories you need to tell may be:

1. The circumstances of your loved one's death

2. The memory of the first time you saw your loved one

3. The treatment your loved one received from doctors or a hospital

4. The financial mess your loved one left behind

5. A description of the funeral/memorial/ash scattering

6. Why your loved one was so important to you

7. Taking care of your loved one through an illness

8. Getting a call or a knock on your door from the police to tell you what happened

9. How well you were prepared for the death

10. How lost you are now or what you will do next

I could go on and on. Your story is your own. I have talked to two people who have lost someone through suicide, and they discovered the bodies. Each said they relived what had happened frequently in their mind before they could say what happened out loud, but they each felt they had to tell their story. And it was a story that people didn't necessarily want to hear. They didn't want to accept that scene into their own thoughts. But their story still needed to be told. Finding an audience that works for you is important. Maybe tell a friend who didn't know your loved one well, or go to a support group or counselor. Or write it out. Just be sure you don't hold on to that story, which will just grow and fester until you have to let it go.

A story I have that was hard to share was when, after a good friend was killed in a head-on car crash, important items needed to be retrieved from the car at the wrecking yard. When I arrived at the yard, I was hoping I could just tell someone what I needed and they would get it for me, but they wouldn't. I had to go the car, the front of which had been crushed into the driver's seat on impact and dig around through blood and broken glass to get what we needed. I couldn't talk about it at the time. What I saw was too horrible to share, so I finally started writing about it in a journal, and eventually the story softened so that it wasn't constantly at the forefront of my thoughts. Sharing helps this softening to occur. I actually hadn't thought about that experience for years before I wrote this, and now I can say it and just remember my friend with love.

How Long Do You Need to Tell Your Story?

Tell your story for as long as you need to. Some people cry every time they try to tell their story, to the point that they can't get their story out. In this case, they need to tell it some more. When your voice fails you or your tears block you, write your story instead. And write it again from a different perspective. The Japanese story "In a Grove," on which the movie *Rashomon* was based, told one story from four completely different perspectives. At the end of the story or movie, the person who read it or watched was left unable to tell which story was the truth. Maybe parts of all the stories were true, while the rest of the descriptions were based on the interests of the teller. You could try this technique when writing your story. Instead of writing it from your perspective, try seeing it from the perspective of an unknown passerby, or of an old friend, or of a police officer who responded, or of a friend who heard about the story later. Write all these stories, then compare them to yours. The more you tell it, the less you need to. Eventually, your story will become your memory that you can hold with love.

Telling your story will also bring out many emotions, and, until you deal with those emotions, you will find yourself telling your story again and again. The emotions you may feel could include abandonment, anger, shock, confusion, stress, or frustration. When Renee's fiancé died, she experienced all of these emotions and would swing from one to another. She couldn't stop telling her story until she worked through each emotion.

Listening to Mourning Stories

Chances are that, in your mourning, you will hear the stories of others. You have become a member of a group of kindred spirits who seek each other out and share. Really listening to the stories of others can help not only the one telling but help you too. Because, in our culture, we don't talk much about death, finding someone who can share the journey with you can be golden. The key here is to actually listen to what the person is saying. Often, when trying to be involved in a conversation, we have a tendency to think about what we are going to say next instead of hearing what is being said. Or we judge what is being said so that we don't really hear the story. For instance, our monkey minds could start rambling on about how our situation is so much worse than that of the person talking, whose loved one had been sick a long time and was old and it was time for him to die. Now I doubt that you would say that to the person out loud, and I doubt that it would do you any good to think it, so just let all those false conversations go, clear your mind, and actually deeply listen to the person who is talking. Look them in the eye, if they will let you, as they speak. Let them know that you hear them, you feel for them, that you care.

If you don't know someone who can tell the story, try searching TED talks, or even YouTube. That way you can listen to people's stories without preparing your own response. You can feel how so many people have been in your shoes. You can experience how death is a part of life, and everyone dies, and everyone grieves those deaths. No one gets through life without losing people they care about. Knowing this, you may not feel so alone or isolated.

The Life Story

We have just been talking here about stories of grief and mourning, but when someone dies, remembering that person's life is also important. I had only known Ron for ten years before he died, and he had lived sixty-four years before me. His mother lived with us for a few years, but she was really living in the past. She was constantly on the phone, talking to old friends about minute details of the parts of their lives they shared, and it drove Ron nuts. He believed strongly in the importance of living in the moment, to the point that he didn't share much about his past. I loved it when he would talk to me about experiences he had or mentors that influenced him. I wish now that I had written down those stories because he didn't repeat them, and I am trying to record for his children what I remember so they will know more about their father.

Memorial services can shed light on the lives of loved ones. At Ron's service, friends came from as far back as grade school, and I learned things I had never heard before. I so wish we could have talked about those things together. I realized that there is much my children don't know about me. Jason, my son, is living with me now, and it seems like every day I tell him some little thing he didn't know about me, and I enjoy that. But in this process, I realize that there isn't much I remember about my parents. I know where they worked and what organizations they were involved in, but I really didn't know them. Taking the time now to write about my parents, to write about Ron, and even to write about me, helps me deal with my feelings and hopefully will give my children a better glimpse of who we are and what they can remember us by. In addition to writing about how you feel, try writing about the life of your loved one, and try writing about your own life.

Exposure to Death

I just saw on the news today that, in the last seventy-two hours, three horrific acts of hate, including the murders of thirteen people and attempted murders of many more, have occurred in our country. Acts of hate, prejudice, and violence are the most frequent headlines wherever we get our news. And video games are common where the goal is to kill as many characters (people) as possible. My son reminded me that the first mass school shooting took place at an elementary school across a busy road from where we lived, and that he and his sister were in lockdown in their classrooms as the shooting occurred. For an exercise in one of my university writing classes, I asked how many students knew someone who had been murdered. Most of them raised their hands, and I realized that I could count five people that I knew. I was shocked. And when I asked if anyone knew people who had been shot, I actually had students stand up to show their scars from bullets. In addition to shootings, we have become numb to instances of car accidents, especially those caused by drunk drivers. And death by domestic violence gets gossiped about, but it goes on.

What does all this have to do with you writing your story? Mostly our society has become blasé about frequent deaths. They always happen to someone else, until they happen to you. When you see these modern-day horrors, write about them. Deal with them. The more familiar you are with a subject, the easier it will be for you to deal with when the time comes. And, inevitably, the time will come, as everyone deals with death in their life. The first death I remember was when Dad picked me up from elementary school to tell me that my grandpa had died. And in the next couple of years, the rest of my grandparents died. My family dealt with the deaths by shielding me from anything to do with them, so I didn't have the opportunity to mourn. Writing your stories of both life and death can help you, and your family, and your friends, to know about who died, and help you all to live your best lives now, knowing that this life is only temporary and we should get the most out of it while we can.

Some Ideas for Telling Your Story

- Write your story like you are telling a friend.
- Write your story like it is your loved one telling it.
- Write your story while listening to your loved one's favorite music.
- Write your story as a love story.
- Write your story as the story of your loved one's life.
- Write your story as if your loved one is dictating it to you after death.
- Write your story about what your loved one would want remembered.
- Write the story of your favorite memories of your loved one.

Ultimately, telling your story acts as a release. Comfort comes as you realize that you don't have to tell the same thing over and over again. When Jacques had his first open-heart surgery, it was a shock. I found that I needed to tell everyone what the whole experience was in detail. I found that, the more often I told the story, the less detail it included. Finally, I wrote the whole experience down in great detail, then I found myself not having to say it anymore. I finally had had my experience, told my story, and was able to come back to the present moment, where healing could take place. Tell your story to whom you want to, but don't feel obligated to tell it to anyone. Explore your story in your journal. Say what you need to say. Then free yourself to start writing your new story.

Practice: Tell Your Story

Out of the many stories you could possibly tell, for now, pick one to write about. You can start by making a list of stories. Consider ones that you spend time thinking about, ones that you can't get off your mind, ones that are the most painful, or ones that are the most joyful. Out of all of these, choose one.

You can write your story as a journal entry, or you can write your story as a short story with a message. Considering what you want to write about will help you to know what form to write it in.

Start by writing a list of all the details you can remember about your story. Be sure to include all the details that are essential to your story. Then string all these ideas into your story. You can share it if you wish, or you can put it away in a safe place so that you can find it later when you would like to read it again.

Keep writing more stories whenever you are inspired. Writing things down helps you preserve details you don't want to lose. You may wish to start a separate journal that is just stories. The more you write, the better you will feel.

Key Tips for Chapter 17

- Don't feel obligated to tell your story to anyone.
- Telling your story can provide relief.
- Take the time to listen to other's stories.
- Start writing your new story.

Chapter 18

Feeling Guilty

"People have a hard time letting go of their suffering. Out of a fear of the unknown, they prefer suffering that is familiar."

—Thich Nhat Hanh

Do you feel guilt related to your grief? Don't be surprised if you do. Just about everyone who grieves also feels guilt related to who died, what caused the death, or the grieving afterward. No emotion has caused me more pain or amplified my loss more than guilt. Guilt is just part of what we do. If we don't have something to feel guilty about, we are good at creating it. Check out this list and see if any of the examples are something you feel, and there is good news. You can do something about it!

- The last thing you thought about your loved one was negative, and you didn't get a chance to change your thinking.

- The last thing you said was hurtful or negative and you didn't get a chance to apologize.

- You didn't insist that your loved one get treatment soon enough.

- You couldn't seem to do anything about treatment you thought was wrong or harmful.

- You didn't visit your loved one often enough or spend enough time.

- You didn't do something you said you would.

- You weren't there at the time of death. You didn't come right away when you were called.

- You didn't notice when there was something wrong that you could have done something about.

- You survived your loved one's death.

- You were happy or felt relieved about the death.

- You were angry at God.

This list is by no means comprehensive. We can experience or make up all kinds of things to feel guilty about. The thing to keep in mind here is that guilt implies an intent to harm. If any action you did or thought you had was not done with an intention of harming your loved one, you are not guilty. Guilt implies that you failed at something or did something wrong, and most of the items on the list above don't fall into that category. As you reflect on the guilt you feel, see if it is about something that isn't bad or wrong at all.

Has someone told you not to feel guilty? That really doesn't help. I know that when someone tell tells me how not to feel, I am most likely to feel whatever they say that much more! When someone says that, just smile and say thank you, then ignore what they said. But sometimes you are guilty, and if that is the case, you do need to deal with that. If you really did make a mistake, like giving someone the wrong medicine which led to their death, or you were driving drunk and had an accident thus leaving someone you loved to die, those are legitimate reasons for feeling guilty. Getting help from a counselor, minister, or support group is essential in cases like these.

Our brains like order. When things are out of order in our lives, we tend to try to get back on track. Consider this when you are looking at things you feel guilty about. When you realize what it is that brings you guilt, examine that and see if, realistically, there actually was something you could have changed, something you could have done differently. In Will Smith's movie *Seven Pounds*, his character suffered tremendous guilt after using his cell phone while driving led to the death of his wife. The movie is about how he dealt with that guilt. What he chose was extreme, making for an interesting movie, but you don't have to be dramatic. You may discover a path to doing something wonderful to help you through your feelings and get things back into order. Candy Lightner's daughter was killed by a drunk driver, so Candy decided to create something that would prevent others from suffering the way she did. Candy is the founder of Mothers Against Drunk Drivers. What could you do or create that would give you something positive to focus on?

In your memory of the experience with loss, is it true? This may seem like a strange question. You say, "Of course my experience was true!" But was it, all of it, really? For instance, when you tell a close friend about your experience, do you say the same thing that you would say to your employer, your mail delivery person, or your daughter? Sometimes we shift the focus of the story we tell and add or leave out details. So which story is the truth? In creating a variety of stories, you may start feeling guilt when you realize how different they end up being. The solution for this is to stay in truth and focus on the positive.

Are there things you would have liked to have done before your loved one died? I would have loved to have spent more quality time with my mother before she died. We hadn't spent a lot of time together throughout my whole life, and after she died, I realized how much I had missed. I knew more about my grandmother than my mom. If I had it to do over again, I would go way back in time and be a better daughter to her, but that couldn't happen, and feeling guilty that I couldn't change anything did not serve me. I had to accept the situation, integrate it into my life by being a better mother, friend, or sister now, while I can, then move on with my life.

This leads to all those things that you could have, should have, would have done that didn't happen. Maybe you could have had a standing date each week with your loved one to catch up. Maybe you could have insisted that your mother get her financial affairs in order. Maybe you would have been nicer to your friend had you known he was going to die suddenly. Maybe you would have been a better wife, brother, friend, employee, or whatever roles you played. Think of all you should have, could have, would have, done, and realize that there is nothing you can do about any of those things now, so speeding time with them does not serve you. Do decide now what you can and will do, then do these things. That will help you release all those old, negative thoughts.

Perhaps your relationship with your loved one wasn't always rosy, and you fall into dwelling on the bad times. Guilt can run wild with telling you that you weren't good enough, that you shouldn't have raised your voice. I went through a period where I kept replaying things Ron said that I didn't like. He would sometimes criticize me in front of others, and that drove me crazy. A friend pointed out an example of that to me, and I dwelled on it for a few days. Now, this isn't something that happened all the time, and he was generally supportive of me, and I know he thought he was being supportive when he would say something like that. I dealt with it by focusing on all the good things in our relationship and realizing that no harm was intended. Then I had to let it go. Stewing about things past would never change anything or bring me joy, and realizing that allowed me to keep things in perspective and move on.

Consider these factors as you explore the guilt that you may feel:

- Guilt is normal. Don't let others minimize it.
- You are not alone. Everybody feels guilt at some time.
- Is the guilt you are feeling the truth? If yes, admit it and deal with it. If not, let it go.
- Are you being rational? You can't control someone else's addiction or mental illness, Alzheimer's, cancer, or anything else.
- Think about who you can talk to about your guilt, then talk to whoever it is. A friend, counselor, group, minister?
- Forgive yourself.
- Do something positive to assuage your guilt.
- Think about what your loved one would say about your guilt.
- Find something good to dwell on.
- What has your guilt taught you?
- Make restitution if there is a way to.
- Know that you can feel good and bad or happy and sad at the same time.

When Ron came home from the hospital the last time, we had arranged for a hospital bed in a spare room that had a bathroom where it would be easiest for the caregivers to take care of him. I am sure he would have preferred to come home to our bed, but there just wasn't room for all he required and for the caregivers to move around him. I was exhausted from having stayed up with him, helping with his care around the clock, for the last week. After we got him settled, I went into our bedroom and just crashed. I could not stay awake. That night I had a dream that he came into the bedroom to wake me up so we could talk. In the dream, his caregiver was standing in the doorway. The next day, I told him about the dream, and he told me that it wasn't a dream. He just wanted to snuggle with me in our bed one last time. I was devastated. He was never able to return to our room, and I felt guilty about that for a long time. Rationally, I know that I wasn't physically able to change that moment. I stayed by his side for the rest of the week, sleeping on the floor, until he died. I think I will always have tears with this memory.

Bonnie shared: "I do not feel guilty about anything in relation to grief. I honor my grief. I actually honor my relationship with grief and how it has led to transformation." How wonderful that that was her experience. If that wasn't yours, that's okay too. Now, just live your best life. Look for good things. Carla's experience was different. "I feel guilty because I was glad Dad died. He was surviving, not living. He was tired of not being able to live his life. He lived three years after the surgery for the blood clot on his brain and lost all of his independence. I felt we did what we could for him, we were there for him, but it was time." Being able to accept this allows Carla to go on with her life and grieve at her own speed. And Brandy said, "It's like a roller coaster for me. Some days are very difficult and others are okay; however, I do feel extreme guilt about not being there for my best friend who passed away." Releasing the guilt you feel about something you weren't able to do can be a challenge, but you can.

I'll bet you feel guilty about something. Something you said or didn't say. Something you did or didn't do. Guilt can be a nasty enemy. You don't need that enemy clinging on to you. Shake it off. Let it go. Do this by forgiving yourself. Say out loud or write down, "I forgive me. I forgive me. I forgive you. I forgive us." Say or write it as many times as you need to. Know in your heart that your forgiveness is done. It is accepted. It is real. And it feels so much better for that nasty creature to be booted out of your life! Kick it out now!

Practice: New Intentions

We talked in Chapter 4 about setting intentions. I set intentions regularly to help remind me to live the way I truly want to. In reading this chapter about guilt, you may have had some tough memories come up that have you feeling or considering some guilt. In order to assuage those feelings, let's write some new intentions. Generally, what you may feel guilty about was not caused by something you intended to do, so the key here is to live intentionally, which greatly lessens the likelihood of having any more to feel guilty about in the future. Intentions that could help with this would be something like:

- Integrity is paramount, so I only speak the truth.

- I make decisions based on the best potential outcomes.

- I constantly give and receive unconditional love.

- What intentions can you write to help you guide your life in the direction you want to go?

Key Tips for Chapter 18

- Guilt can seriously obstruct the grieving process.

- Reasons for feeling guilt can be examined.

- Releasing guilty feelings related to the relationship with the person who died, or to the actual death, must be explored and dealt with to move forward with grieving.

Chapter 19

Living in the Moment

"The purpose of life is a life of purpose."

—George Bernard Shaw

The concept of mindfulness is basically living in the present moment. We cannot live in the past or in the future. The only place we exist is right now. Acknowledging this reality can bring a peace and calmness into our lives. When dealing with loss, we often ruminate on the past, thinking of how things were when our loved one was alive. While we have many pleasant memories, when we ruminate, we are often spending time dwelling on how things will never be the same and that we deeply miss our loved one. We also frequently face the future with fear. How can we survive alone? What has happened to our financial security? Will we ever feel better than we do at this moment?

Becoming mindful, you will recognize that time is an illusion. What you remember from the past may or may not be true, depending on how you recall your experiences. If you were in a car accident, you may have a need to make the other vehicle at fault when, actually, it could have just been

an accident. To come to terms with your past, you may make
yourself a victim in order to justify your actions to yourself.
Or you may do the opposite. You may think of your loved one
as perfect after he or she is gone, while you actually know
that all was not. For example, maybe he never remembered
your anniversary, or she always used up all the hot water.
When being mindful, you can look at the past objectively and
remember that what happened in the past is a memory, not
your reality right now.

Living in the moment and being mindful are trendy terms
right now, but don't dismiss them. They actually are the
truth. Consider that the past is over and that the future is not
guaranteed. All there is left is the present. Consider where
you are and how you feel right now. You may spend time
considering your past by thinking of all the things you should
have done, would have done, or could have done. Yet you know
that none of those things can be changed.

After Ron died, I spent much time thinking about the
decisions that we made during his illness. I had told him how
hard dialysis was for Jacques, and how I don't want to go on
dialysis myself if the need ever arrives. When we had those
conversations, Ron would say he didn't want to go on dialysis
either, but when we got the phone call saying that his lab
test results were critical and that he needed to start dialysis
right then or die, we decided that he would start dialysis and
we could talk about it later, when we had time to consider it
all. But after he started, they explained that stopping meant
death. We did know that before he started, but it didn't seem
real. We ruminated about that decision a great deal, and after
he died, I had a hard time letting it go. Ruminating like this
is perfectly normal, as long as you can eventually let it go.
Right now, it does not serve me to regret the decision or feel
responsible for it. I accept the decision as what we felt was best

at that moment. The decision cannot be changed, so I no longer dwell on it.

You also can spend time longing for the past. While I can remember much joy I have experienced, dwelling on not being able to still experience that same joy does not serve me. Special experiences we had, like traveling, entertaining, and moving to Maui, were wonderful, but I cannot relive them. At first, I longed for his voice, his touch, his kiss, and so much more; knowing that I cannot have these experiences again can either make me sad or cause me to treasure the experiences and be grateful to have had them.

And while you can't live in the past, you also can't live in the future. Worry and anxiety about what may happen later today, tomorrow, next year, or sometime in the future just causes pain. You may worry about having enough money to get by, being alone for the rest of your life, or pleasing others by doing what they expect from you. These worries can make you a slave to the future. How you react is a choice. Choose to treasure the memories.

It is impossible to not think about what happened in the past or what you would like to happen in the future, but the key is to not dwell in either situation. Create a balance of past and future, but spend most of your time in the present. Right now. Becoming aware of living in the moment can feel challenging. You may feel anxiety or uncertainty, but by committing to recognizing your mindfulness, you gradually will become comfortable with your situation.

How to Live in the Moment

First of all, get rid of your expectations about how you think things will be. Be open to change and release all negativity or fear you may have about living in the present. You will discover that this practice releases stress and actually leads to better health. Here are ideas to get you started. Don't feel you have to do all these things at once. Choose one or two, and when you get comfortable with them, try some more. Be gentle with yourself in this process, and keep in mind that change is inevitable. Make the most of it in the ways that are best for you.

- **Unplug.** Escaping into watching television or playing games on your phone or following the news on the computer can suck up lots of time. Doing some of this may be relaxing and good for a break, but be mindful of how much time you are actually spending hooked up to something electronic. There are apps that monitor screen time. If you try one, you may be amazed at how much of your life you are wasting.

- **Savor.** Regardless of what you do, take time to enjoy and benefit from the whole experience. Instead of eating a bag of cookies, eat one or three and put the rest away in portioned-out baggies. Don't do anything else while you eat each one. Focus on how good each cookie tastes and how good it feels in your mouth. Savor all that you do, not just food. Enjoy each experience.

- **Breathe.** Of course we all breathe, but take the time to experience your breaths. Take time each day to find someplace comfortable and do nothing else but focus on your breathing. While waiting for an appointment or waiting for the oven timer to go off, sit and take slow, deep breaths, filling up your abdomen and then your chest. Hold your breath for a moment, then slowly release. With each breath you take in this fashion, you will find yourself more relaxed.

- **Listen.** Often, when we are in a conversation with someone, instead of really listening to what they have to say, we spend the time while they are talking planning what we will say next. Instead, focus on who is speaking. Look the person in the eye, smile, and really hear what they are saying. When they stop talking, then decide what you will say next. You will discover that you remember more of the conversation, and the experience could be less stressful than if you are always competing with the other person or focusing on yourself.

- **Meditate.** Meditate each day for at least five minutes, and try to meditate longer than that whenever you can. Always find a comfortable place where you will not be disturbed. Make a practice of silencing your phone and turning off any distractions. Choose the form of meditation that serves you the best in each situation. I enjoy anything from spending a quiet five minutes in my back yard between tasks to going to a sound meditation, complete with crystal bowls and gongs.

- **Do less.** When you make a to-do list at the start of your day, choose the top three items on the list. Do those three things and don't think of anything else until they are complete. Then, if you have time, choose three more. Don't try to do everything at once.

- **Eliminate worrying.** When you discover yourself worrying, stop. Worrying about anything does not serve you. Examine what you were starting to worry about and consider how to eliminate it. Instead of worrying about whether you will be able to get into your favorite restaurant, make a reservation. Instead of worrying about having enough money to make it through the month, create a budget. Anything you can worry about, you can also discover a solution for.

- **Make simple tasks a meditation.** Try focusing on the moment when washing dishes by hand instead of in the dishwasher, being conscious of each step. Enjoy the motion. Enjoy the warm water. Or, when sweeping the porch, make each stroke deliberate. When pulling weeds, feel the sun on your back, smell the fresh earth being uncovered. Watch the earthworms, ants, or bees do their tasks.

- **Smile.** Most often our faces are in a neutral position, or maybe even a frown. Consciously recognize when you aren't smiling, then smile, looking at people you encounter. You are likely to receive smiles in return, which feels so good.

- **Love what you are doing.** If you don't love your job, find one you do. If you don't love who you are with, find someone you do. If you do not love the exercise you are doing, change your routine. Whatever you do, find the joy in it and focus on that.

- **Practice forgiving.** Holding a grudge takes much energy. When you let go of whoever or whatever is bothering you, you have more room for love and joy, and you are likely to help someone else feel better in the process.

- **Focus on the present.** When you are concentrating on what you need to do tomorrow, you are not giving the attention you need to for whatever you are doing today, right now. When your mind wanders off, bring it back to what you are doing. When you are spending time with your children and worrying about what you need to do after they leave, you will have missed a precious gift.

- **Be kind.** Give a stranger a compliment. Open the door for someone. Bring in your neighbor's trash can when you bring in your own. Make a double recipe of your favorite casserole and give one to a friend. Offer to go to the drugstore for an ailing friend. Think about something you would love someone to do for you and do that for someone else.
- **Avoid judgment.** Just because someone doesn't do something the way you think they should doesn't make them wrong. If your friend has different political beliefs, change the subject or be kind in your discussions. What someone else wears or how they cut their hair doesn't matter.
- **Release addictions.** Addictions are actions done automatically without thought. If you feel that you drink too much alcohol, try cutting down gradually. If you can't seem to stop playing solitaire on your phone, limit the number of games you play each day and find something constructive to do instead. Whatever your addiction, if you cannot seem to stop on your own, seek help.
- **Be mindful of how you do things.** When actors perform in plays for a long run, chances are their performances will lose its authenticity. When the number of performances is limited, chances are each show will be fresh. Keep your actions fresh. When you do the same thing the same way for too long, chances are it will not be enjoyable. Find a way to keep it real or try doing something else.

- **Practice empathy.** When you are empathetic, you understand and share feeling with another. After my husbands died, I discovered an empathy for other widows, which expanded to others who have lost loved ones, no matter what the relationship. By being there for others, I provided comfort and listening, both of which help me feel better too.

- **Put space between things.** Finish what you start, then take a breath before your next task. Do each task deliberately. When you rush through things or don't put your best effort into what you are doing, whatever you have done loses its value. Take your time with what you are doing and take a break between tasks.

- **Eliminate.** Being surrounded by stuff can be suffocating. Look around you. What can you release? You may have outdated files that can be shredded, or clothes you will never wear again that you can donate to the women's shelter. You may have way too many mugs or trinkets. Let go of anything you don't use or need. The space that appears when things are released can be freeing.

- **Flow.** Go with the flow of what you are doing. Being in the flow is when you are so lost in what you are doing that you don't realize time is passing. I recently took a drawing class where I would be shocked when the class was over. I became so involved in what I was doing that I had no idea time had passed. I have also experienced this when working out, when swimming, when doing ceramics, when reading a book, and when cooking. Find where you can slide into the flow and enjoy every moment.

When I asked people how they practice mindfulness after having lost a loved one, their answers varied. After Carla had back surgery, she said she would "sit in the back yard feeling the sun on my back and looking at the plants and the artwork. I was not able to do anything but relax into it and appreciate the world around me and just let myself slow down." Taking time to just relax is an essential luxury when healing.

Patti says she has always lived in the moment, as much as possible. "Today. I make a point to go on nature treks—at those times, I am just there, enjoying nature, spirituality, all of life. It is a great time to reflect and remember. But I tend to focus on the moment, more often than that, by trying not to worry about the future. In unexpected traffic delays, being antsy and driving recklessly will not help matters. I just figure, this is the drive today, and I will arrive when I arrive." I love how she recognizes that she is living in the moment instead of worrying about the future. Letting go of worrying brings peace.

Ellis is a comedian, and he comes up with his original material by paying attention in the moment. He listens to what people say, for those words can spark an idea that leads to a routine. Beyond finding humor, listening can allow you to recognize shared experiences so that you discover that you aren't alone in your feelings or experiences.

Bonnie recalled a time in the first year of her grieving. "I spent an afternoon at an arcade that also had ping-pong tables with a bunch of friends. It was maybe three to four months after my husband died and, for the first time since he died, while playing ping-pong, I was 100 percent present, laughing, and not thinking about the past or the future." That's in the moment! Living in the moment for me usually involves an extreme emotion and some sort of physical activity.

Benefits of Mindfulness

By finding ways to simplify your life, you will discover that you spend more and more time in the moment. Releasing past worries and experiences and knowing that I am on the path to a wonderful future has allowed me to live mindfully. Mark Twain said, "I have known a great many doubts, but most of them never happened." Do you spend time regretting the past or worrying about the future? Most of us do to a certain extent, and when you recognize that you are doing this, you can release this practice and lighten your life. Be mindful.

Practice living in the moment. Saying "If only I had done more, had been there, had tried harder" doesn't help anyone. Instead, in this moment, know that everything is good, is love, is beautiful. Dwelling on past experiences only makes it difficult to move on. Worrying about future experiences won't make the future clearer or better. Staying present in the moment is your pathway to peace. What are you doing right now?

Practice: Mindfulness

Do a mindfulness meditation. Plan on taking some time for this. Find a quiet, beautiful place where you will not be disturbed. Get into a comfortable, supported position so you won't be bothered by how you are sitting. If you are inside, dim the lights. You may want to light a candle or some incense. Start by completely relaxing your body. Take a slow, deep breath, feeling it down to your toes, then, as you release your breath, release the tension in your toes. Continue taking slow deep breaths, focusing on releasing all of the tension in all of your body, one part at a time. When you are entirely relaxed, focus just on your breathing. Slowly breathe in. Hold your breath. Slowly breathe out. Hold your breath. Continue breathing in the relaxed state, focusing only on your breath. When you feel your meditation is complete, slowly come out of your deep relaxed state, tensing and releasing muscles to wake them up. Stretch a big stretch and smile a big smile.

Plan to do a peaceful, mindful meditation often.

Key Tips for Chapter 19

- Dwelling in past experiences only makes it harder to move on.

- Worrying about future experiences won't make the future clearer or better.

- Remember the importance of living in this moment, where everything is good, is love, is beautiful.

Chapter 20

Following Your Bliss

"Follow your bliss and the universe will open doors where there were only walls."

—Joseph Campbell

Our parents are usually our first examples. We learn by observing and mimicking them. Then we go to school and observe our teachers and incorporate what we learn from them into who we think we are supposed to be. And we are surrounded by so many other examples. We watch our friends, we watch television. We watch our electronic devices and movies. We are stimulated in every direction we look, and it is up to us to pick and choose from all this the pieces that we put together to make our vision of ourselves.

This vision is likely to change many times over the years. When I was very young, I was impressed by my Aunt Mona, who was a nurse. She was always taking care of us, she was kind, and she always smiled. I also closely watched Linda, my older sister. She was beautiful, had a boyfriend, and was going to get married and be a wife and a mother. I always loved art and observed artists any time I could. My parents were very active in service organizations and always had leadership roles, so I saw that these things were important, too. As a young adult, I worked at putting all these bits and pieces together to see how I could mold myself into the person I thought I should be.

Throughout life, I tried so many paths. I always thought "if only" I accomplished the next goal, got the next degree, got the new job, found the right husband, raised my children, became the leader of whatever group I was in, served my community, became a nurse, became a teacher, became a writer, published books, participated in the theater, then I would be fulfilled and my life's work would be accomplished. In all that, though, each time I reached an "if only" goal, I just discovered there was another one on the other side. And this was good. I gained many skills, had great experiences, learned much, and served many, yet I always knew there was something more. My learning and skills built on each other and served me well. But I knew there was more.

In searching for what I was supposed to do next after Ron died, I realized that I had always been living a life of me and someone else, or of being who I thought others thought I should be. I had never really lived on my own, just me, as me. As I examined my life and my passions, I started a path of self-discovery. This led to my realization of my passion for the arts, not just one, creating and appreciating. It opened me up to my joy of writing. Though I have taught writing for many years and have written textbooks on the process itself, my epiphany was that I really love to write, not just talk about it or teach it. I also uncovered my sincere desire to serve others. This awareness ultimately guided me to join these many fragments into the goal of helping others in a positive way. I realized that all of those experiences I had and things I learned have guided me to my life's purpose, my bliss.

In the process of writing this book, I also used the skills I used at the university to create online classes in a new way so I could teach others how to reclaim joy after loss. I also learned how to create a YouTube channel, using lots of the skills I learned in the theater. From all the art and design I have done, I find joy in designing classes and my website. From the community leadership work I have done, I used my skills to form a group and to teach writing classes to grievers. I recognized that I was well-prepared to care for both Jacques and Ron as their health declined because of my work as a nurse. I realized that all that I have been doing in my life has led me to my ultimate life's purpose, which is to serve you in navigating through your loss in every way I can. It is my pleasure to be here for you.

So, what is your bliss? How do you discover it? First, discover what brings you joy. Think of all you do, all the experiences you have had in life—which of them make you smile the most? What are you doing when you feel most alive? What have you always wanted to do but haven't yet? What skills do you have that you would like to develop? Who would you like to serve? What would you like to learn? How would you like to be served?

Much of our lives have been focused on the basic needs of having food, clothing, and shelter, and assuring that our families have those things too. But there is so much more to life. Maybe you think that you should be living differently, that your life isn't enough. The good news is, you are alive, your actual life is enough, and you can actually do whatever you want to. The path to arrive at knowing this is by committing to the responsibility for your joy to you, only you. No one else can give you joy and happiness. Be being awake, by being grateful, by setting your intentions, by writing your affirmations, you actually can manifest your heart's desire. Make a commitment to follow your bliss.

Once you commit to your bliss, you will be surprised at the doors that open for you. You will have new experiences, some better than others. If something occurs and you say, "Oh, no! This isn't what I wanted!" recognize that whatever is happening is something on your path and see what you can learn from it. How can this experience serve you? If you are still challenged by the experience, release it and move on to the next experience. Holding on won't bring you the bliss you desire, but letting go can make way for new opportunities. At one point I was employed in a job that I loved to do, but the environment where I worked was toxic. I chose to release that job, and a much better one opened up for me that I hadn't ever thought of before. Had I hung onto the job that caused so much stress, I would have deprived myself of my wonderful next opportunity.

Practice being mindful, paying deep attention to what is happening when you feel the best. Then seek opportunities that provide the opportunity to experience this feeling again. The more you feel like this, the more you will be drawn to what provides you with the experience, and you will be following the path to your bliss. To find these opportunities, open up to taking risks, to doing new things, going new places, meeting new people. If you stay stuck where you have always been, chances are, you won't experience change. Committing to the road less traveled does lead you to new destinations.

When you start on your path toward your bliss, if you really pay attention, you will discover things along the way that show you are going in the right direction. You may experience instances of synchronicity. Synchronicities are unexplainable instances of coincidence. One experience I had was when I traveled from Maui to Los Angeles. The airport at LA is huge, and there are many vans available to give you a ride to the rental car offices. I had rented my car from a small agency, so the van was very small, too. When I got on the van, there were only two other people, and one was my dear friend Kate, who I hadn't seen in years. She had traveled from Tennessee and would not have been on that van if her flight in Tennessee had not been delayed eight hours! Another instance came the first time I attended a group here on Maui where people had discussions on all things related to death. I came with a friend but didn't know anyone else in attendance. One of the people in the group had questions about funerals. On my way to the meeting, I had received a phone call from a friend on the mainland who told me about Chap's funeral, which had been held that day. It had been a day-long festivity that even included the USC marching band. I shared with the group about this amazing event, and when I was finished, the man next to me asked me the name of the person the funeral was for. When I told him, he told me that Chap had been his fraternity brother and that he hadn't heard that he had died. In both of these instances, there was no way I could have anticipated them. And I started paying attention and realized that, especially since I moved to Maui, I have synchronicity experiences often.

On your path to bliss, other things that you may experience are increased energy, feelings of happiness, a sense of direction in your life, and you may even realize your life's meaning. That's lots, I know, and it is all completely possible. The main thing is to be paying attention so you can appreciate the experiences when they come, and you can see your pathway to bliss.

So now that you basically know what bliss is, and you want to commit to following your bliss, how do you get started? I tend to be organized and want to put things on my to-do list, but bliss is not one of them. But here are some things you can do to start your process of discovery.

- **Be mindful.** Mindfulness is basically bringing your attention to the present moment and staying there. This is the biggest step in the process of finding your bliss. Bliss only exists in the present moment. You can't plan on experiencing it tomorrow or in the future.

- **Remember what brought you joy in the past.** In thinking about that, can you experience joy like that now?

- **Pay attention to when you are experiencing joy.** How does it feel? What are you doing when it happens? Do you always have this feeling when you are doing something similar?

- **Explore new possibilities.** I love taking art classes and getting totally lost in them. Maybe you have always wanted to do yoga or Pilates. Or maybe you'd like to learn to bake bread. Or maybe you'd like to write poetry or travel. Think of something new and different for you to try.

- **Say Yes!** If you receive an invitation, accept it. I have discovered so much by doing this. And don't worry if you aren't receiving invitations now. When you commit to saying yes, opportunities to say yes will appear.

- **Be curious.** What would you like to know? I am learning about Hawaiian gardening and Hawaiian history to become acculturated to my environment. I've been reading books that I have wanted to but didn't make time to in the past. I just read Viktor

Frankl's *Man's Search for Meaning*, and I am so glad I did. My reading gives me perspective on my path.

- **Focus.** By writing your intentions and your affirmations, and writing in your journal daily, you can keep focused on the direction you want to go. Step boldly into the unknown. Document your journey along the way.

- **Love, trust, and honor yourself.** Self-care is so important when you venture into new territory. Take good care along your way.

- **Be uncomfortable.** So often we fear something different. Let that go. The more you allow yourself to experience new things, the more likely you are to discover what you really love.

- **Share your bliss.** When you find your path, you'll love to share. Your bliss will help others decide to discover theirs. And sharing feels wonderful. I love to publish my blog and my classes, and I love to interact with my students. And I am thrilled that my book is available to help others. All this brings me so much joy, and I definitely follow my bliss.

Take some time to explore all of this. Recommit to really writing your intentions, affirmations, and your journal. Discover you own very personal pathway to bliss!

Practice: Blissful Meditation

Now is your opportunity to explore your bliss. First, follow the suggestions from the chapter about writing your intentions and affirmations and writing in your journal. Then do a beautiful, blissful meditation. Find a peaceful spot where you can sit undisturbed. Tune into some soft spa music. Close your eyes, breathe deep, and focus on the word *bliss*. If your mind starts to wander, pull it back to bliss. This is not thinking about bliss. Rather, you are experiencing the peacefulness and joy of bliss. Repeat this meditation often, until you find yourself immersed in your bliss.

Key Tips for Chapter 20

- Search for your bliss.
- Discover your bliss.
- Follow your bliss.

Chapter 21

Accepting Invitations

"The art of acceptance is the art of making someone who has just done you a small favor wish that he might have done you a greater one."
—Martin Luther King, Jr.

After Jacques died, I spent almost a year in isolation. I would go to work and come home and be by myself. People who I had been social with before disappeared. I felt like a black widow. Now I realize that people who had known us both didn't know what to say or do, and without realizing it, they didn't want me to rain on their gatherings. Jacques died in February, and when the new year rolled around, I immersed myself in reflection and decided that I just couldn't go on living this lonely life. In considering what I could do to improve my situation, it dawned on me that I could accept invitations. Up to that point, I hadn't been getting invitations, but they started to come in, and I started doing things I had never thought of before.

I was asked to join the editorial board for the newspaper. We met with a wide variety of people, from legislators, to businesspeople, to community leaders who would pitch ideas for the newspaper's support. I learned so much in this position, and even had the opportunity to write an editorial myself on an issue that I felt strongly about. Then I was asked to be on the board for the planned unit development where my new home was located. By doing this, I was able to meet many neighbors and help solve issues that we all were affected by.

My daughter convinced me to start going to her trainer to help me get into shape. Joe Petersen is an ultramarathon bicycle racer, and he asked to be the nurse for his bicycle racing team. On my first race, the driver didn't show up, so I ended up driving the follow car for close to twenty-four hours straight across the desert. What an adventure! We won and set a record, so he asked me to go on the Race Across America, another amazing opportunity.

I was getting good at saying yes, so when the Film Commissioner for my county invited me to accept a grant to create a film festival, I said sure. Again, I met fabulous people and learned so much. None of those things had even been in my dreams before, but I did them all. I met new people. I provided needed services and input. And I enjoyed every moment!

I invite you to look at invitations differently. I realized that if I sat feeling sorry myself because no one invited me to do things, the invitations weren't going to come. Like the old saying, "Be careful what you wish for," what I was doing was reinforcing that invitations didn't come to me. When I shifted my focus to be open and receptive to new experiences, my world opened up. Consider how you would really like your life to be. What have you always wanted to try? After you have some ideas, do something about it.

I realized that I didn't want to spend my first Thanksgiving alone after Ron died, so I invited everyone I knew to come to my house for dinner. Many had family or traditional plans, but many others were thrilled to have somewhere to go on the holiday and to get a home-cooked meal too! Some people

contributed their favorite dishes, which was special for
them, and we ended up starting a new tradition of having my
home available for holidays. Now I know I won't be alone for
holidays, and I'll find lots of joy in the process.

Take a moment to think about all the people you know who
don't live far away. Who can you think of who might be alone
and hoping for someone to call? What kinds of activities could
you do together that you would really enjoy? For instance, there
is a lovely park not too far from me that I thought would be a
great place for a walk. Then Shena called me and said that her
friend Adesina wanted her to go for a walk there, but she was
busy, and asked if I would like to go for a walk with Adesina.
I ended up having someone to walk with, and I found a new
friend in the process.

I host a weekly gathering at my house where neighbors come
together to share fruits and vegetables that they raise in their
yards. One week, Sharon came and introduced herself. She
lives only a couple of blocks away and was a recent widow, so I
told her about the work I am doing, and we ended up becoming
good friends. Through going to activities with her, I've learned
much about farming and food insecurity that we deal with
living in Hawaii, the most remote place on earth. And I've met
new people through her. I told Sharon how much accepting
invitations helped me, so she started accepting invitations too
and loves the results.

You may receive invitations you don't want to accept.
That's okay, and it's normal, but before you just say no to an
invitation, take time to think about it. Why do you not want to
accept it? If the person who invites you is someone who you are
not comfortable with, it's logical to say no, but first consider
what is making you uncomfortable. Maybe the person is always
sad and needy, and you don't want to be surrounded by doom
and gloom. I wouldn't accept that invitation, but I would turn

it down gently to not add to the person's sadness. Or maybe the person is always in a good mood and you aren't sure how you will react when you feel your life isn't happy. Being around that positive energy might just be the perfect thing to lift you up. Take a deep breath, smile, and say yes, while keeping a positive attitude the whole time. This may be just what you need to turn a corner.

When you say no often enough, invitations will dry up, so carefully consider this when you are deciding what you want to do. People may interpret your saying no as rejection. They may think you don't want to be with them, and people do get their feelings hurt. If you do pass up an invitation and regret it, try inviting the person to something else (even to go out for coffee) or writing them a thank-you note. This can help you both feel good and maybe lead to more opportunities. Patti said, "I did not always feel like going out, but I did. In part, it was because I knew that is what my loved one would have wanted." Getting out with others always helped. Sharon didn't really want to make the effort to go out or do new things, but since I told her how accepting invitations changed my life, she says yes right away to new opportunities.

Instead of just waiting for invitations, try inviting people to join you. Sometimes people will say no to grieving people because they fear being around someone dealing with loss. That's okay. Invite someone else, and someone will say yes. And don't write off those who say no. Remember to invite them again, sending them some love and support now. Maybe saying no to you was hard for them, and they'll appreciate you reaching out again. Marjorie has this example: "After my husband died four years ago, several friends invited me to go on a trip to the coast with them. They pooled their resources and took me on a carefully planned trip, paying for meals and all. We took long walks, inspected unfamiliar areas, and generally had a wonderful three days together. Of course, I accepted their invitation to go do something together, and the memory of their thoughtfulness right now is still profound. Moving away from the center of our own darkness into a circle of light made up of friends can help us heal. When I miss the feeling of being loved by my husband, I can remember the love of these caring people toward me."

This would be something great to arrange with friends!

Isolating yourself is an easy trap to fall into. Pay attention and notice if you start doing this. If it's been a while since you have talked to someone, make a phone call or invite someone over. If you feel like you don't have anyone to talk about your feelings with, reach out. I resisted going to a group because I thought it would be just sitting around with people who were all wrapped up in their own issues and had no reason to care about mine. Then someone told me about a Death Café, so I went to one, and I am so glad I did. We met at a Mexican restaurant and had chips, salsa, and margaritas and talked and laughed and cried a little too. This proved a wonderful outlet for me. I liked it so much, I am now the facilitator and cherish the new friends I have met in the process.

See if there is a group that suits you. Or you could start your own by inviting some people you know who are dealing with loss. I started a group where I teach writing related to issues of loss. I have been a writing teacher for many years, so this group gives me an opportunity to use my skills to help others, and we are all enjoying the process. I also offer classes online and a closed Facebook group where we talk about dealing with loss in a positive way. I'd love to have you take classes or join the group. Try searching online to discover groups you may resonate with. In Facebook or Instagram, try searching with words like "grief" or "widow," and you'll find lots of results.

One challenge that often occurs is that you and your loved one probably did much together, and the friends you interacted with thought of you as a couple. Couples often don't invite singles to join them. If you were used to doing activities based around your child and the child dies, you may have the same issue. And you may not feel comfortable around these people either. If this is the case, be on the lookout for different opportunities. Be open to meeting people whose situation is similar to yours. I discovered a group of ladies in an organization I belong to who would get together at each other's homes for dinner. I didn't know they were doing this until they invited me to join them. I was the only widow. The others were happily single, and one new friend was a nun. I enjoyed their company and was grateful for the invitation. Maybe you could create your own little dining group, or walking group, or activity group. This can be a stimulating activity to learn and do new things like going to art galleries, or classes, or concerts. Just have fun and explore.

With all this talk of things to do with other people, do remember that it is fine to spend time alone, too. You don't have to be with someone else to find peace and joy. Just love yourself, smile, and feel your joy. And when you do spend time with others, just say a big yes to new adventures and see what comes up!

Practice: Create an Invitation

What is something you would like to do, or someplace you'd like to go, or someplace you'd like to dine? Who would you like to do one of these things with? For instance, there is a new exhibit at the aquarium here on Maui that I hear is fabulous. I can figure out who I'd like to go with and invite them. And I love to go on walks here on the island. I went on a beautiful walk before with Julie. I could invite her to go on a walk to a different place. And I've been wanting to go to the Monkey Pod Kitchen in Ka'anapali, so I just need to ask someone and go! Or you could invite some friends over to discuss a book or make cookies. Or you could search the Meetup app and see what's going on in your community where you can meet new friends.

Start by picking one thing and invite someone you would like to spend time with. And say yes the next time someone extends an invitation to you.

Key Tips for Chapter 21

- The value of accepting invitations.
- Saving no is important when needed.
- It's important to be involved.

Chapter 22

Transformation and Preparation

"My compass always points north."

—Rev. Joanne Coleman

The saying that there is nothing certain in life but death and taxes isn't quite true. The other certainty is loss, and we all experience loss many more times than our death or our taxes. Your loss may be as profound as the loss of your husband, wife, or child, or it may be a smaller loss, like the loss of your notebook or your ability to drive. Loss comes in many forms, and it can plunge us into the depths of depression, or it can provide us with the opportunity to reassess our lives and discover things we have never considered before. I see loss as the opportunity for change, for looking at our world through a different lens that will allow us to grow and discover the best life we can lead.

Grief provides us with transformation and preparation for the rest of our lives. You are a new you because of a change that you didn't expect, didn't want, and couldn't plan for.

Allow yourself to experience your memories of your loss and contemplate where you really are in your life now. How are you transforming? Where are you right now? Based on what you are experiencing and learning from this process, where will you go now? What is your passion? What do you really love?

Let's look at the process of transformation. Transformation can be thorough and complete, like the caterpillar into a butterfly. Or transformation may be on a smaller scale and be slow and gradual. Transformation starts when your loss occurs. Whether your loved one's death was sudden or occurred after a long illness, you can't know what you are going to feel like when it happens until after it happens; then, everything is drastically different. Your transformation is the process of what happens starting at that time. At the time of loss, you probably felt alone, empty, and in a fog. We all have some of these feelings. When the fog starts to clear, then questions start to arise, and the first one is frequently, "What do I do now?" When you recognize this, you can start to come to terms with your new life. This process isn't quick and may take years, or even the rest of your life, and that's good because you see that you are actively participating in making your life the best it can be. Here are some areas to consider as you contemplate your transformation:

- Organizing the practical matters of life, such as bill paying, can give you a sense of relief and security. Create a schedule for when bills are due. Also create a schedule of when annual items need to be attended to, like insurance renewal, car license renewals, and tax payments. Also have a schedule for birthdays and other dates you want to remember.

- Recognizing that there will be times you will miss your loved one more than usual and preparing for that when you can. Any anniversaries or special events that you shared may trigger deep feelings. Take special care of yourself at these times. Do something special just for you. You may want to plan to be around loved ones, or you may want some time to yourself. The key is to recognize what is happening and deal with it gently instead of ignoring your feelings.

- Working through your feelings that come up. You may be self-critical because you think you should have done something differently related to your loved one's death, or you may feel some anger arise at unresolved issues you were having. Take the time to examine things as they come up and deal with them. For instance, if you are feeling sorry that you didn't get to apologize for something you thought you should have done, write a letter to your loved one and pour out your feelings, then forgive yourself and release the situation. Holding onto things that happened or didn't happen in the past does not serve you. Bring your focus to the present.

- If your emotions having to do with your loved one are confused or conflicted, spend some time with this. Write in your journal about these emotions, then consider what you can do to deal with them.

- Reaching out for help may be good for you. Often, we try to just deal with things on our own, but in a time of loss, becoming overwhelmed can happen. Ask for help if you need it. Talk to a trusted friend. Find a good counselor but be sure to get recommendations of who to go to from people you trust. Find a support group that works for you. A support group can be as simple as a few friends sharing dinner or coffee, or as structured as a hospice support group. Find the best help to suit you and your needs.

- Finding ways to deal with pain. Pain can be physical or emotional or both. If the pain seems physical, get it checked out by a professional. Often simple measures can help without medication, like acupuncture, massage, physical therapy, or simply getting moving, like going for a walk. People suffering loss often find it hard to move, to get up off their chair, but moving is vital. The more you walk, the more you will be able to walk, and the better it will feel. Be wary of dealing with your pain by using drugs or alcohol. At a time of loss, you are especially susceptible to the misuse of either or both of these.

- Trying something new can open new opportunities for you. Maybe you have always wanted to travel, or play golf, or take dancing lessons, or plant a garden, or learn to sew, or play an instrument, or go hiking. Now is the time to try. You can focus on one thing or try a variety of things you have wanted to try and then decide which one you want to spend more time with.

- Exploring your creativity can bring much joy. Do you have something creative you loved to do in the past? Try it again. Or find a class to take. I've been taking lots of classes, like ceramics, drawing, jewelry making, printmaking, weaving, and painting. I've done some of these things before, while others are totally new to me. And I like them all so much that I haven't decided where to really focus yet.

- Finding new relationships is healthy. You will find that some friends you have had may fade away, so now is a good time to discover new friends. To do

this, you need to go where people are. That may
sound simple, but so many people stay at home alone.
Make a list of all the places you would like to go and
start going. There is no rush, but each time you meet
someone is another step forward.

- Dealing with conflict in old relationships allows you
  to release old disagreements that no longer serve you.
  Start by considering what the conflict is. Is it worth
  pursuing? Do you want to apologize? Or maybe your
  friend doesn't even know that something is bothering
  you. If you feel this is the case, answer these three
  questions, then decide what to do. 1) Does something
  need to be said? 2) Does it need to be said by me? 3)
  How can I say it with love?

- Getting comfortable with your new role in life. Before,
  I was Jacques's wife, or Ron's wife, or the professor's
  wife, or the minister's wife. Of course, I had many
  other roles, but I no longer have these roles. I spent
  time discovering what my role in life is now and how
  to adapt to it. What is your role now?

You'll discover more things to consider as you are moving
forward. Make writing in your journal about things like this a
priority to help you through and a place to remember what you
want to work on. After Ron's death, I spent some time in the
limbo of that fog. When I started to emerge, my main though
was "Okay, now what do I do?" I had completely devoted my
life to spending every moment with Ron, not just for physical
care, but so we could enjoy each other's company. This precious
time was a remarkable experience, a real high point in my life,
and when it was over, I was really lost. I realized that I needed
to discover what my life's purpose was then. I first took stock of
my skills and interests. I continued to do things I loved, reading

primarily, and keeping an open mind that I would discover my purpose in due time. When Chappy died and I created a year's worth of note cards for his wife, which led me to the inspiration to write this book, I realized that I had discovered my purpose. I have the opportunity to love and support people who are on the path to reclaiming their joy, and this is so rewarding to me. I love facilitating group meetings, teaching writing classes, teaching online classes, writing and speaking about reclaiming joy, and I am so grateful to have been open to this inspiration when it came.

Now is the perfect time for you to examine how you feel about yourself, consider what you would like to change, prioritize goals for your life, and define your life's purpose. Much work has been done examining the process of transformation, and there are surprisingly many methods. The ultimate goal of all the methods is the discovery of the best way for each individual to deal with their journey of loss leading to the best possible new life. As we learn to consciously recreate our reality, we can step into joy we might not have imagined we could have without paying attention to the process. Sound good? This is entirely possible, and you may already be in the process without having thought about it. You can have and do anything you want. Follow your bliss. Go for it. Right now.

Practice: My Transformation

Take some time now to explore how you are changing in your journal. What roles do you play now? What are you doing that is new for you? What do you want to be doing? How are you actively participating in your transformation? You can consciously create your reality, so step forward into the life you desire.

Key Tips for Chapter 22

- Your life is different today than it ever has been before.

- You are playing new roles in your life now.

- You can consciously create your own reality.

Chapter 23

Regret

"Life is too short, time is too precious, and the stakes are
too high to dwell on what might have been."

—Hillary Clinton

My parents lived about an hour away from us, so, when they
were traveling, they would stop to see us. We would usually
meet at a restaurant for lunch or dinner. One day they called
and asked us to meet them, so I went. My daughter, who was in
high school and busy, breezed in for a moment but just said hi
because she had someplace to be. That turned out to be the last
time we saw Daddy. And my daughter was devastated because
she had not told him she loved him that day. Since then, she
doesn't end a conversation with someone she loves without
telling them so, but sharing all that love cannot bring back
that opportunity she missed. Her grandpa knew how much she
loved him, but that doesn't help assuage the regret she feels.
Observing this caused me to pay more attention to what I say,
and to not leave things unsaid whenever I have the opportunity.

Everyone who experiences loss has some form of regret.
Sometimes we misidentify it as guilt, and it is important to

make the distinction between the two. Guilt comes after we consciously do or say something hurtful. Regret comes from recognizing things we feel we could have or should have done. In the case of the death of a loved one, most frequently we will deal with regret.

Jacques's best friend John had been celebrating his fortieth birthday all day. We had all gone to a big dinner honoring him for the service he had been providing as the president of the teachers' union for the college district he worked for. He lived about an hour away from us, so we had him come to our house for coffee. He spent quite a while with us, talking to my high-school-aged children he was close to. When he decided to leave, we all tried to convince him to spend the night before his long trip home. He told us that all the coffee we gave him had done the trick, and that he was fine. Half an hour later, we received a call that he had been in a head-on collision with a semi-truck and was killed instantly. For a long time, I felt guilty that I had allowed him to drive when he shouldn't have. I finally realized that I didn't allow him to drive and did everything I could to convince him not to. But I will always regret that he got in his car that night.

Regret comes from feelings about what we think we could have or should have done, and it also comes as the result of procrastination. In one week when I was thirteen, my father had exchanged our home for a failing business that he was sure he could revive. Because of this, we had to move into a small house on the property of the company. And that week my sister had her second child in a community an hour away. I had a terrible nightmare about my grandmother that week. I told my mom I was afraid for my grandmother, and she just told me we were all under pressure because of the business, losing our home, and my niece being born. I called my grandmother. She didn't answer, and this was before answering machines. I asked my mother if we could go see Grandma, her mother, but she said she was too busy. I kept asking. She kept saying no. Four days later, Mom decided to go to Grandma's house. She lived alone and didn't leave her house much except for church, so Mom was finally worried. She found that she had died in her bed sometime within the last four days. I was so angry at my mother, but I didn't tell her because we were all devastated by Grandma's death. In this case, my grandmother probably would have died anyway, but Mom and I especially felt regret for not listening to my intuition, and Mom's procrastination made a difference in how things turned out.

Jacques suffered renal failure when he had to have anesthetic used during surgery to repair his broken hip. Because of a reaction to the anesthetic, he had to go on dialysis. We didn't know what that would entail, and it was a grueling, miserable experience for him for the remaining six months of his life. He didn't tolerate it well due to his heart failure and diabetes and was absolutely miserable. I told Ron all about Jacques and all he went through, and he told me that he never wanted to go on dialysis if it ever became necessary. I knew he was serious, that he was comfortable with his mortality, and I supported his decision. And then there was an emergency. His nephrologist was at the airport on his way out of the country for vacation, and he checked on lab work from some of his patients while he was waiting. He knew Ron's feelings about dialysis and had told him at his last visit that he was doing well and that talking about dialysis was in the distant future, but that's not what his labs said.

Ron's labs were so bad that he was not likely to live to the next day. It was a weekend, so I suggested that we go to the hospital to get the lab tests repeated, since they were so drastically different. We went, and he was rushed into the emergency room. They insisted that he had to have procedures done and they would talk afterward because they had copies of the labs the doctor had seen. He went along with them because he thought he was buying time so that he could get some answers. And that was the start of his being on dialysis for the rest of his life. The whole situation was so complicated, and we were so frustrated. We believed that, since we had informed the doctor of his wishes and we had it in writing, his wishes would be followed. We both experienced so much regret over how everything was handled. In hindsight, we could see what we should have done along the way, but that didn't help us.

Before Ron died, we had deep discussions about his dialysis and the complications along the way. There were many. He asked me to follow through to do what I could so that others would not have to go through anything like he did, and I promised him I would. He had major complications from the peritoneal dialysis they ultimately put him on that he could not tolerate. I spent months writing letters and talking to anyone I could get to listen about what could be done to fix the system that had failed him. I cannot tell if any changes have actually been made, but all of the providers have been informed of the situation. I could not just regret what happened. I had to do all I could to make it better for the next person.

When I asked Julie about regrets, she said, "Regrets? Of course, But I don't camp there. I have to turn it around. Example: my stepfather loved baseball, and I wanted to go to a pro game with him and my kiddos. It didn't happen. So now I am thinking about taking the kids to an Angels game and using it as a time to remember him and just have a good time at the ballpark."

I love Julie's approach of celebrating her stepdad now instead of regretting what didn't happen.

Rachel says that she only has one regret with Jimmy. They had unfinished business to do with one another, but she was afraid to speak up, and that fear haunts her. If anything like this is bothering you now, do something about it while you still can. Bambi told me that her biggest regret was the pain she put her dog sitter through because, when Bambi's home was destroyed by the huge Thomas Fire in Ventura County, the firefighters could not allow the dog sitter in to save Bambi's dog. While Bambi did not cause any of this, she still has feelings of regret.

Contemplate circumstances that you have dealt with related to your loved one. Take some time to make a list of things you feel guilty about and things you regret that can be from omission, commission, or procrastination. Actually write your answers. Consider things that could fall into these categories:

- Things you wish you had done differently
- Things you wish you had said
- Things you think you should have known
- Things you feel you should have done
- Things you wish you hadn't done
- Decisions made over medical treatment
- Feeling like you took your loved one for granted
- A situation left unresolved
- Missed opportunities
- Things you intended to do but didn't get the chance to
- Doing something you wish you hadn't
- Feeling that you enabled behavior that led to a death
- Any other regret you can think of

This is a heavy list. Just reading the list can be hard, and harder still to consider your answers. Living with regret over anything related to your loss can devastate your life. And you can actively work to make things better. Start by looking at each response you wrote. Then deal with each one individually. Ask yourself:

- Is this something that is a reality in my life right now?

- Is this something that can be changed?

- Is this something I actually want to change if I can?

Your answer is likely to be no to all these questions. And that's a good start. Now you can work to deal with what you experienced. Do this process for each of the regrets you wrote down.

- Focus on this present moment in relationship to the regret.

- Release any feeling you have of blame against others.

- Release any feeling of blame you have for yourself.

- Apologize to anyone you need to.

- Forgive yourself, practicing self-love.

- Decide if there is something you can do now to make the situation better.

- Release the specific regret you are dealing with in this process.

- Express your gratitude for your release.

Remember that, in this process, you are doing it for yourself. You cannot change how anyone else feels or deals with the same situation. You are your priority here. When you take care of yourself, you have room left to practice compassion toward others. Whatever you did, or perceived that you did, in relation to your loved one's death does not make you a bad person. You are a perfect, beautiful, wonderful soul deserving of your complete forgiveness.

In all this talk of regret, you may be not thinking about all the things you did right. We all have a tendency to worry over regrets and things we consider failures while we tend not to celebrate what is right and good with our life experience. I spent the last two years of both Jacques's life and Ron's life not working at a job outside our home and focusing on them. I cherish each of these moments and am grateful for the experiences. I have wonderful memories, and I am using all I learned in the process now to help others deal with loss and to find joy. For me, this is something I celebrate and express my gratitude for. For you, look beyond any kind of regret. Focus now on the good of your life in this moment. Focus on what you learned and what you can do to make the rest of your life the best it can be. Focus on being the person your loved one loves.

Practice: Release Regrets

Using the process in this chapter, make a list of any regrets you have, and go through the process of releasing each one individually. After you release each regret, write what you learned from the process and how you commit to your life being different now. Take your time with this deep process, which can bring your clarity and peace.

Key Tips for Chapter 23

- Discover currently held regrets.
- Mend or fix past regrets.
- Work to currently live without regrets.

Chapter 24

Becoming Aware

"There is power within you that is always greater
than the condition before you."

—Rev. Johnnie Coleman

Enjoy your transformation, using it to expand and grow.
Enjoying loss may sound like an oxymoron, but think about
this a bit without judgment. By experiencing your loss, you
are becoming more fully aware of life, of life's value, and life's
brevity. When you recognize this, you naturally open up more
to your life experience. In seeing each moment and living right
there in the moment, the pain of the past and the uncertainty of
the future are no longer priorities. Just recognizing the beauty
and grace of the moment brings you endless, deep, genuine joy.

Someone is always saying something like, "Time heals all
wounds," or "Just be patient. You will grieve less over time."
While there may be a little truth here, just sitting and waiting
for the time to be up so that you can feel better will never work.
To get to a point where you are ready to step forward, work on
looking at how you feel right now. Are you ready for things to
be different? Letting go of the heaviness of your feelings can be

a challenge. If you feel your feelings are holding you back, ask yourself these questions.

- **Is there a different way I could look at my loss?**
  When something comes up, spend some time with it
  and see how you feel. For example, if you would really
  like to try a new restaurant but you hesitate to go
  alone, you could either ask someone to go with you or
  go alone, committed to enjoying the experience.

- **If I think of something that will help me move
  past where I am right now, will I do it?**
  Talking yourself out of doing something that would
  serve you is an easy trap to fall into. If you come up
  with something that will help you, just try it and see
  how it works out.

- **Can I talk about what's holding me back?**
  If you recognize what the issue is, try talking to a
  trusted friend about it. Or bring it up in your support
  group or with your therapist. Often, just saying
  something out loud will help you see exactly what you
  need to do.

Ultimately, you will discover that you have been moving forward on your path. You start discovering who the new you is in this new role in your life, and joy is coming to you in this self-discovery process. You will come to an understanding that "grief" doesn't heal. If you have been trying to heal your grief, try instead to heal your feelings about grief. Grief doesn't heal, just like your reason for grieving doesn't miraculously go away, but you can feel better. Start taking responsibility for your joy, for living your best life. Imagine for a moment that you were the one who died, and that you could look back at your loved one and see how he or she is doing. Would you be devastated to see that person in constant pain, crying, and unable to adjust to life without you? Now reverse that scenario and see yourself as you know your loved one would want to see you. You'd be smiling, involved in your life, your family, your community. You would be healthy and active. Now think about what you need to do to make that vision come true.

A great place is start is by living in the present moment. This practice was the biggest gift Ron gave me. We didn't dwell on the past or things we could not change. We also did not dwell on the possibilities of the future, when chances were that I would be without him at my side. By staying in the moment, we were able to find peace and joy in all we were doing. Is this how you live now? Look at how much of each day you spend thinking about how things were before. Then think about how much time you spend wishing and hoping about how you would love for things to be. Dwelling in these thoughts is perfectly normal for some of your time, but as you strive for that time to be less and less and for you to spend more time in the present moment, you will discover a lightening of spirit where life becomes easier, less of a burden, and where there is room for joy to rush in.

Rachel described the process she is going through by saying, "I wouldn't say I'm moving forward. And I'm not stuck. It's more like a labyrinth or a winding yellow brick road. There are days when I don't miss any of those who are gone, and some days when I miss all of them. Something will remind me—a song, a story, or a moment—or some other trigger will get me going and the tears might flow. The difference now is that I move as quickly as possible toward gratitude. I don't get stuck. I think how lucky I am to have shared time with this amazing person!"

Bambi has discovered that she is moving forward through her loss. "One of the biggest ways is to no longer take a back seat to who I am. I am not fanatical, just quietly giving no excuses or apologies for the core essence of what make me...me."

When you do your daily meditation, add this to your practice. Start by asking yourself a few questions that will allow you to become centered and ready. Ask yourself, "Am I here right now?" If not, release whatever thoughts you are feeling or thinking that are pulling you away from being peaceful. If things are pulling at you, like how you are going to pay the bills or if you are going to be alone for the rest of your life, before you meditate, get out your journal and write about what's bothering you. Create a plan if you need to. Examine what you are thinking to see if it really is true. Can you do something about what is troubling you? Once you write all this out and discover how to deal with it, go back to start your meditation. You will discover that you can more easily go deeper into meditation, which will calm and restore you so you can have the energy to move forward when you are finished.

At this point, are you experiencing your authentic self? Throughout our lives we play so many different roles, some we enjoy and thrive with, others not so good. You've played roles like a child, a daughter or son, a student, a worker, an activist, an entrepreneur, a mother or father, a volunteer, a friend, a relative, a leader, a follower, and many more. What roles are you playing right now? You may be in several of the roles I listed, but you also may be a widow/widower, an orphan, a grieving person, a single person, a depressed person, a happy person, an energetic person, a beautiful person. What roles are you playing right now? Some roles bring despair, while others can bring joy. Right now, it is up to you to define who you are at this point in time. When you are clear about your roles, then you can decide how you want to address these roles. For instance, if you realize that you are an orphan, who can you turn to as a role model or a father or mother figure? What would you like to talk to this person about? What activities would you like to do with this person? Question each role you play and create a plan for how to address that role.

Consider other roles you may be playing. Are you a people-pleaser who always wants to be the best and look the best? You say yes to things you really don't want to do. You dress to please others. You choose activities based on what someone else likes to do. Carefully examine this and see if this is what you really want to do, or if you are behaving so as to please others or maybe to make yourself invisible to others. Or maybe your friends and family feel that you have come into money as a result of your loss, and wouldn't it be wonderful to give them or loan them some money? Grieving people are often taken advantage of by well-meaning friends and family. Allowing this to happen may make your future difficult without needed resources, so be sure you are making financially responsible decisions and get help when you need to. You may also be feeling that you have to keep yourself busy, that any alone time is too much to bear, so you keep active to the point of exhaustion. Recognize if you are doing this and find a way to slow down. Take some time here to consider who you really are, who you have been, and who you would love to be. Develop a detailed plan of what you need to do to actually be who you want to be.

After Ron died, when I was ready, I discovered that I didn't know what to do next. I spent time journaling and meditating and considering what my passions are. At first, I didn't feel passionate about anything, and I felt adrift. I made a conscious decision to be open to what I was meant to be doing, where my heart could soar. Through the journaling I was doing exploring this, I realized that what I really love to do is write. I wrote more. And in that writing, I saw that I could inspire others to gain comfort through writing. I have been a university writing teacher for years and have written textbooks on writing, so this seemed a logical project for me to work on. What was different now is that I saw how my writing and teaching could deeply help others going on this journey with me. The more I do this work, the more people I touch, the more hugs and smiles I get from them, the more reassured I am that I am fulfilling my life's purpose with something that brings me and others great joy.

Where are you in your journey now? Look back on the past year. Consider each month separately. How did you feel? How have you been changing? Are you where you want to be at this point in your life? If yes, how can things be even better for you? If not, what do you need to actively do to improve your life? This I know: Each moment can actually be better than the one before. As you work to discover what the truth is about where you want to be, you can actively take steps to move forward to that goal.

Discovering what your purpose is right now gives you something to focus on and gives you constructive things to do, so now think carefully about the rest of your life. Here are a few things to consider:

Live your highest and best life without worrying about what others think. I had such a hard time when I started dating Ron. Our relationship felt so right and wonderful to me, but I was so concerned about what everyone else would think. I felt that I was viewed in the community as Jacques's wife and that people would think I was somehow betraying him by going out with someone else. I also kept thinking about the marriage vows of "Till death do you part." I didn't feel like I was suddenly not a wife when Jacques died. That role had been mine for so long that it was very difficult to give up. I realize now that what anyone else thought was not any of my business, and they may not have been thinking what I thought they were at all. This transition took a while for me. Thank God Ron was patient.

Moving into a new relationship did not mean that I had to forget Jacques. At first, Ron called him my ex-husband. I explained to him how much that term bothered me. He was my husband who died, or my former husband. I stayed in touch with Jacques's children and grandchildren and still consider them part of my family. Ron even performed the wedding ceremony for Jacques's granddaughter. I now speak with love about both Jacques and Ron as I loved them both deeply, though the relationships were entirely different. Honoring the fact that, when someone dies, the memory of them lives on and keeping that in perspective has helped me move forward in my life with love.

Patience with yourself is a virtue to practice. Some days you will feel lonely and miss your loved one so much, and other days you will feel fresh and grateful for the new you that you are stepping into. Know that you can dwell in that space of the new you, and be kind to yourself when you get a little down. You are stronger than you have ever imagined, and those beautiful new days will become your new normal.

Know there is no one-size-fits-all timeline. If one of your friends never seemed to rise up from deep grief and another friend didn't seem to mourn at all, neither story refers to you. For you, each step you take is forward. You will feel what you feel when the time is right for you, so you don't need to be concerned about what anyone else thinks of as normal as related to your process. Just take care of you.

Remember that you are not a victim. I used to always want something or someone else to be responsible for how things turned out for me. When I learned to let that behavior go and started knowing that I am the only one responsible for my life,

I felt a huge weight lifted from me. Actively, consciously, live your best life.

We all die, and the more prepared we are, the easier it will be for us and those we love. Having been through the process that death brings with your loved one, you learned much. How can you apply what you learned in preparing for your own death? I learned from having to clean out my mother's house that I have no intention of leaving lots of stuff behind. Each day now I find things to release that I can give to someone who could use or enjoy whatever it is, to donate it to charity (I think I single-handedly provided a room of books for the Friends of the Library), recycle what I can, or just plain throw things in the trash. Also, getting all my financial and legal affairs in order brings me great peace of mind.

The biggest lesson of this chapter is for you to enjoy your life now, every moment of it. Do only what you really want to do. Be only who you want to be. And above all, live your life in love, especially for yourself.

Practice: What Now?

Writing intentions helps you to focus on who you are and what you want to do. After reading this chapter, what have you become aware of that you hadn't been thinking about before? Considering this, what do you intend now that is different than how you were living before your loss, and how you were living before you read this chapter? Write three clear intentions which indicate the new you, your new direction. Refer to these intentions a few times over the next few days and see how they are affecting your life. Then write more intentions as your guide.

Key Tips for Chapter 24

- Enjoy your life.
- Do what you want to do.
- Live your life in love.

Chapter 25

Forgiveness

"Instead of forgiving someone else for anything,
forgive yourself for judging them."

—Maggie Hood

A major life lesson I have learned is the value of forgiveness.
Holding onto judgment or anger does not serve you. Take
some time to consider everyone you may hold something
against. Maybe they were not honest with you. Maybe they did
something to hurt you. Maybe they judged you. Whatever they
did, how you react to it is up to you. Carrying around anger and
judgment does not serve you and can feel like a heavy weight on
your shoulders. For each thing you come up with, consider the
source. Recognize that the person who hurt you may not even
realize what happened. Release any negative thoughts you have
toward this person. Really let it go. Keep doing this until you
realize that you live in a state of forgiveness. This is so freeing.
Your life, your thoughts, your love, are only your responsibility,
and living from the perspective of love rather than judgment
and anger feels amazing!

In talking with Ron, I realized that I had spent most of my life holding some level of anger toward many people and situations, and all that did was make me irritated. When I started examining who and what I was upset about, I discovered that, frequently, what was bothering me was my problem, not someone else's. This took me a while to come to terms with. I found this definition of forgiveness that helped me: "A willingness to abandon one's right to resentment, negative judgment, and indifferent behavior to one who unjustly injured us, while fostering the undeserved qualities of compassion, generosity and even love toward him or her" (Enright et al. 1998).

What this basically says is, let it go, whatever it is. But don't just stop thinking about the issue; rather, actually pardon it without resenting what happened. I can hear you saying, "That's easy for you to say," but no, it actually isn't. When I really felt someone had done me wrong, the easy thing would be to get angry and just know that how I felt was all their fault. What was hard was to recognize my role in what happened, or alternatively, recognize that I had nothing to do with what happened.

The biggest instance of forgiveness that I have had in my life was when Ron went on peritoneal dialysis. He had been doing well on hemodialysis, but he had to go twenty miles away three times a week to sit in an environment of very sick people who sometimes died while he was there. The peritoneal dialysis could be done at home at night as he slept, which sounded wonderful. However, right from the start, we knew something was wrong. He had a whole team taking care of him, including doctors, nurses, a social worker, and a dietitian. We started reporting problems right away, but all those people didn't really listen to us or would hand us off to someone else on the team. As he declined and had more and more unusual symptoms, they brushed it off, saying they didn't think it had to do with the dialysis, but they offered him nothing for relief of all that was happening. When he realized he was coming close to death, he asked me to be sure that I pursued his situation to help make sure that others would not have to endure what he did. Six months after he started peritoneal dialysis, he died, and we both were sure that all the symptoms were caused by an intolerance or allergy to the dialysis solution we pumped into him every night.

As hard as it was, I spent months writing letters, making phone calls, and giving depositions. I received apologies from his local doctors, but the dialysis centers and the manufacturers of the solutions said they would look into it, and I didn't hear anything else after that. Several people suggested that I sue for wrongful, negligent death. I spent much time in meditation and prayer about this and realized that I had done as I had promised Ron. That if I won a suit, it wouldn't bring him back or really help anyone. Reporting everything I could to all those involved was the best I could do, and my hope was that they honestly pursued the situation. After all was done, I looked at everything and realized that I did my best. I knew the doctors didn't intend harm. I knew the hospitalists were overworked and undertrained for all the circumstances they came up against. And I realized that the rest of his team did their jobs to the best of their ability and knowledge. I decided to forgive them all. Releasing the anger that had been boiling beneath the surface ever since the problems started was like a miracle. I let it all go, and in the process, I felt great relief. I could breathe easier, sleep better, and even smile. This experience helped me put my whole life in perspective. It changed how I would look at and how I would deal with things that came up.

So how does forgiveness work? First, you need to recognize who or what needs to be forgiven. When you identify the situation clearly, the next step is to pardon whatever happened. The key here is to do this without holding any resentment. This can be the hardest part. I saw an episode of *60 Minutes* which showcased a project done by the University of Wisconsin's Law School where they introduced perpetrators of violent crimes to people who were victims of these crimes. I was especially touched by Angel Wendt. Her brother had been killed by a drunk driver who had previous drunk driving convictions. When her brother died, her life of being a schoolteacher, wife, and mother was turned upside down by her rage against the man who killed her brother. She had a difficult time facing her own life, and in an effort to ease the pain, she decided to participate in this restorative justice project five years after her brother's death. When she met Lee Namtvedt, who was serving time for her brother's death, she discovered that she and Namtvedt were both crying because of their sadness over her brother's death. When this happened, she found a need to forgive him, and when she was able to do this, her life changed. The weight of her anger lifted. Her desire to be a good mother, teacher, and wife all returned. She knew that her forgiveness did not change the fact that the accident happened or Namtvedt's guilt, but it did allow her to forgive herself for the feelings she had been carrying. Her ability to forgive this person under these circumstances is a beautiful example of the power of forgiveness.

While practicing forgiveness does give you the opportunity to decrease depression and anxiety, it also allows you to increase hope. Take some time to examine your life and make a list of those situations and people that you could forgive. When I did this, I was surprised at how long my list was. I realized that I could not change hurtful things that had happened. I also saw that some of the things on my list weren't entirely rational. As I went through my list, I did some journaling, examining exactly who and what the problems were, and discovered that sometimes the problem was my perception of what happened. I looked at any place where I was holding resentment. I realized that I had spent much time in victimhood, having chronic feelings about situations that I could not change. One by one, I worked through the items on my list. Some things were a challenge to let go, but oh so worth it when I was ready. On other situations, I would get stuck knowing there was nothing good or right about what happened and that a person was responsible for it. These things took longer to work through. I would ask myself what it served for me to stay angry or upset. When my answer became that it would not serve anyone, I could see that I could let it go. And this practice changed my whole perspective on life.

Know that refusal to forgive someone is an action. You are making a conscious decision to not let something go. If this is the case, I encourage you to reevaluate your feelings. Getting stuck in the loop of unforgiveness does not serve you or the person who needs forgiving. This situation can become chronic and snowball, making the situation much worse for you. This is especially hard when the feeling you hold is toward your loved one who died. This happens often. An example in my life was when Jacques had to have his first heart surgery. We discovered at that time that he was also diabetic. After the surgery, he made a commitment to eat well, which was a challenge for him as he loved the pasta, cheese, meats, and wines from his Italian heritage. But he stuck to his commitment. He lost much weight and was able to get entirely off of insulin. He was exercising and loving life like he hadn't in years. Then, gradually, he started eating more, and eating foods that weren't in his best interest. As the weight went up, the exercise went down, the lab tests got worse, he had to go back on insulin, and the situation got so bad that he eventually had to go on dialysis. I was so angry. I did not tell him, though. I figured he was making his own choices and the results were his problem. But they were really our problem, and they led to his death. For a long while, I let that anger I had been holding back come forward. However, after much deep work on myself, I realized that much of my anger was at his loss and his lack of a good life his last few years. When I got to that point, I saw that I needed to forgive him, and to forgive myself that I didn't work more to support him in making good choices when I still could have. When I finally was able to forgive both of us, I felt so much better and was able to release all the negative feelings I had been carrying around.

In addition to forgiving others, be sure to practice self-forgiveness. I know I have done things I am sorry for, and when I recognize that, I actively forgive myself, usually by writing in my journal. I keep track of what I have done so that I can remember not to repeat a behavior that does not serve me.

When you practice forgiveness, know that forgiving does not condone what happened. For instance, though I truly forgave Jacques for not taking care of himself and not eating wisely, that doesn't mean that either of those actions are okay; rather, that I forgave him for doing them, and I continued to love him unconditionally. Also, when you forgive someone for something they did that harmed you, the fact that you have forgiven them does not mean that you need to continue your relationship with that person. For instance, I had an employee who did whatever she could to destroy my business. She lost her case in court and I forgave her, but I did not choose to hire her back. I understood that she was a troubled person, and that I didn't recognize that before I hired her initially. I learned from this too, that I needed to more thoroughly check someone out before I hired them. And I forgave myself for not doing this in the first place.

One thing that can be a great help in moving forward is to focus on living a life without so many situations you would need to forgive. When you change your attitude toward yourself and others, you will see how much better your life is. Ron taught me to be impeccable with my word. I didn't realize that I wasn't, until he would notice me saying something that was a big exaggeration, like I used to do for effect. He would say, "Was what you just said true?" And of course, it wasn't, so I would say, "I take that back," and restate what I was trying to express with complete truth. Doing this exercise caused me to look at what I was saying all the time, and as I did, I realized I could be doing so much better! I did, and this brought me a lightness of heart that I still enjoy without regrets.

I encourage you to examine your opportunities for forgiveness and to release all that does not serve you. You will be so glad you did!

Practice: Forgiveness Letter

Consider who or what you haven't forgiven in your life. Actually write a list. Take a couple of days to do this, because you are likely to keep thinking of different things. From this list, choose one thing that you consider the most important thing that needs to be forgiven. You may need to forgive someone who is living or dead, or you may need to forgive yourself. Write in your journal exactly what the circumstances of the situation are. Once you have clearly defined what you are going to forgive, write a letter of forgiveness where you completely release the responsibility of whatever happened. When you complete your letter, mail it if you can. If the letter is to you, put it in a safe place where you can refer back to it if you ever feel you need to. Then, let it go. Whatever it is, don't spend time thinking about it anymore. Then write in your journal what

it feels like to have released this situation. If you have more
things to forgive, repeat the process until you notice that you
have given up assigning responsibility to others or to yourself
when things don't go how you wanted them to.

Key Tips for Chapter 25

- Forgive everything and everyone you need to.
- Let go of whatever you have forgiven.
- Release being a victim of your circumstances.

Chapter 26

Surviving and Thriving

"And when great souls die, after a period, peace blooms, slowly and
always irregularly. Spaces fill with a kind of soothing electric vibration.
Our senses, restored, never to be the same, whisper to us. They existed.
They existed. We can be. Be and be better. For they existed."

—Maya Angelou

We have been through this journey together through twenty-six
chapters. During this time, you have had highs and lows, and
you've made discoveries that were beyond your imagination
before you picked up this book, the biggest of which is that life
didn't stop. Life does go on, moment by moment, and in each
precious moment, more light, more beauty, more joy has the
opportunity to enter your life when you allow it.

You learned to wrap yourself in love as you navigated
through the early mourning that comes with the devastation
of loss. By being patient and being open, eventually, in your
own time, you started the discovery of what your new life is
now knowing that things will never be the same, but they can
be equally as beautiful and filled with love, if not even more so.
You have put your affairs in order and learned to take special
care of yourself on each step through this journey.

You have learned much about the importance of gratitude and you express it freely by writing it in your journal and thanking people every time something comes up that you are grateful for. You are experiencing the joy that these expressions of gratitude bring into your life.

You are constantly migrating away from your loneliness into a life filled with self-love and lack of judgment as you discover ways to serve others on their journeys. You have discovered what true joy is, and you seek it out and express it at every opportunity that comes your way.

You have discovered books and people and groups to support you on your way. You are becoming part of your new community of friends. You have let go of possessions and thoughts that no longer serve you, and you have replaced them with the freshness of new ideas and beauty, changing your living space to reflect the new you.

You have developed your own spiritual practice where every day you write down what you are grateful for, you write in your journal, you meditate, you write the intentions and affirmations you use to guide your decision-making, and you express the joy that you experience every single day.

You have released giving value to judgments others make of you as you have embraced how you love yourself. And you have released feeling guilty, replacing it with feeling loved and blessed in making your best decisions. You experience your grief healthily while keeping it in the best perspective for how you live your life now. You give yourself permission to do exactly what you want, knowing that you can manifest anything you desire.

You have discovered the beauty and joy of each moment and have committed to allowing that to guide your way as you plan your future and follow your bliss. You consciously decide what you want to do, whether being creative with art, music, or dance, or being creative in your career, focusing on how you can best serve others and yourself.

You have started accepting invitations and find great joy in discovering ways to play, celebrate, and love your life. You have cried many tears, and still do when you need to, allowing them to refresh your spirit to be ready to begin again. You have forgiven yourself and everyone you need to for any perceived slights, allowing yourself a fresh slate to move forward from.

You revel in all the wonder, awe, and amazement you can find, which allows you to be open to all kinds of love. You have come so far, and you are amazing. I am grateful you chose to go on this journey with me. I look forward to hearing from you and sharing your experiences and your joys!

"There will come a time when you believe everything is finished. That will be the beginning."

—Mark Nepo

Afterword for *Loving and Living Your Way Through Grief*

by Melo Garcia

Congratulations. Yes, I am congratulating you. You have just read so many different ways to help you to navigate through your journey of grief, through your journey of loss. And it hurts. And it's impossible many days, but it's worth it, to find your way to live. Not to exist, not to wait. But to find living after the loss. When I met Emily virtually, it wasn't entirely because of grief. Yet we spoke for hours about the similarity of the way we both view grief and loss, yet I yearned for her peace and her calm. I began to study her, I devoured every morsel of her website, and her journal course she gifted me. And as I started not only to practice journaling but to create ways to find living each day, I found the ability to grieve and to live, and it wasn't one or the other. I found myself feeling again, and I was so attached to feeling only emotions related to grief and loss; it was a welcome and needed opportunity to utilize the exercises and theories Emily gave and continues to provide me!! We often create an expectation of what grief looks like, and as Emily highlights throughout the book, we must decide to allow the living to change and become new. And then, a few months before publication, she gave me the manuscript of this very book you are reading. I sat and read, nodding at every word, in tears of gratitude that these words will live in this world forever, helping all of those who have grief and loss. Grief and loss aren't meant to be cured or diagnosed but felt, worked through, and the result is to live. To live in peace and to live and to grieve. Emily is a one-of-a-kind soul, yet this book has been left for you to devour or to nibble as you are able. This book is meant for you to give to anyone who you see face grief and loss. And the whole meaning of this book isn't sadness and death, but it is, in fact, one of the greatest love stories you'll ever read; it's a story of love that is infinite. It's your love story, and it's my love story, and most importantly, it is Emily's love story. If grief was a language, Emily writes and speaks it fluently and without question has helped you to create the steps you need to find your way. She brilliantly advises only to do what you can when you can, and maybe that's to pay this book respect.

Melo Garcia, Grief Mentor,
LFMT AfterChloe.com

Gratitude

So many people contributed to the fruition of this book. The inspiration was provided by those who have been on the journey of living, transitioning, and loving me through it all. To my husbands Rev. Ron Threatt and Jacques Thiroux, who valiantly lived every moment to the fullest. To Yvonne Demetriff, Shena Medley, and Robin Garrison, who loved and supported me on the way. Lori and Chap Morris for their love and inspiration.

I am eternally grateful to my agent, Meriflor Toneatto, who guided me through the process of creating this book. And many friends contributed their experiences: Karen Brown, Patti Ross, Marla Iyasere, Ellis Wynne, Karyn Shaudis, Nancy Edelhertz, Brooke Brown, Maryann Michalski Cord, Annis Cassells, Lynel Johnson, Saundy Sparling, Cathy Butler, Carla Stanley, Bonnie Neubauer, Rev. Rachel Hollander, Julie Sherwood Bumatay, Kelly Maple, Bambi Poindexter, and Jeanette Richardson Herring. Many other friends and family inspired and supported me: Fontaine and Mike Huey, Rose and Sophie Rabinov, Willie and Michelle Davis, Linda Robinson, Stephen Thiroux, Jennifer Adrian, Katie Thiroux, Matt Witek, Rickie Byars, Rev. Greta Sesheta, Rev. Deborah Johnson, Michael Bernard Beckwith, Saffronia Threatt, Yusef Alexandrine, Anhthu Li, Dawn Wade, Henry Blenner, Maggie Hood, Jason Thiroux, Abigale Auffant, Sharon Toutant, Ryn Kapahulehua, Kimokea, Adisina Ogunelese, Adrian Antonescu, Alexis Witek, Bodhi Be, Christine Burke, Debbie Adams. Guinevere PH Dethlefson,

Mila Poaipuni, Isabel Thiroux, Gina Satriano, Jeanette Hablewitz, Jeff Zimmerman, Joe Petersen, Justin Kauflin, Orville and Hazel Lofton, Pam Galbraith, Ron and Julie Metoyer, Sydney Thiroux, Shea Derrik, Kevin Kastle, Shirley Brewer, and Tom Faught.

My intention in writing this book is to provide love and support to anyone who is on this journey with me.

About the Author

Emily Thiroux Threatt is a lecturer, author, and speaker with extensive personal experience in the grieving process due to the deaths of her two husbands, as well as her father, mother, aunts, uncles, and many friends. She has learned to face life with love, optimism, and joy. In turn, she has created a unique program called "Writing Your Way Through Grief" to help others through the grieving process.

She holds a master's degree in English with a Concentration in Writing. She has been teaching writing and composition on the college and university level for over thirty years. During that time, she wrote three writing textbooks, published by Prentice Hall and Pearson Education.

She participated in the Bereaved Person's Association in Bakersfield, California, which her husband Jacques Thiroux cofounded. She also assisted her husband, a bioethicist, with multiple revisions of his popular text *Ethics: Theory and Practice*, published by Prentice Hall and Pearson Education.

Emily conducts workshops, speaking engagements, and retreats on transforming from loss to joy on the mainland of the United States and in her home on Maui, Hawaii.

To learn more, please visit her website at: lovingandlivingyourwaythroughgrief.com.

Mango Publishing, established in 2014, publishes an eclectic list of books by diverse authors—both new and established voices—on topics ranging from business, personal growth, women's empowerment, LGBTQ studies, health, and spirituality to history, popular culture, time management, decluttering, lifestyle, mental wellness, aging, and sustainable living. We were recently named 2019 and 2020's #1 fastest growing independent publisher by *Publishers Weekly*. Our success is driven by our main goal, which is to publish high quality books that will entertain readers as well as make a positive difference in their lives.

Our readers are our most important resource; we value your input, suggestions, and ideas. We'd love to hear from you—after all, we are publishing books for you!

Please stay in touch with us and follow us at:

Facebook: Mango Publishing
Twitter: @MangoPublishing
Instagram: @MangoPublishing
LinkedIn: Mango Publishing
Pinterest: Mango Publishing
Newsletter: mangopublishinggroup.com/newsletter

Join us on Mango's journey to reinvent publishing, one book at a time.